D0890099

MEDITERRANEAN LANDSCAPE DESIGN

Thames & Hudson

Louisa Jones

photographs by Clive Nichols

MEDITERRANEAN LANDSCAPE DESIGN

VERNACULAR CONTEMPORARY

With 265 colour illustrations

CONTENTS

JACKET
Photograph of Louisa Jones courtesy Beatrice Pichon.
Photograph of Clive Nichols courtesy Clive Nichols.

PAGE 1 Wooden walkways at Argentario in Tuscany;
landscaping by Paolo Pejrone.

PAGES 2-3 Al Hossoun in Morocco, designed by
Arnaud Maurières and Eric Ossart.

OPPOSITE La Malherbe on the French Riviera,
designed by Mireille Ferrari.

First published in the United Kingdom in 2012 by
Thames & Hudson Ltd, 181A High Holborn,
London WC1V 7QX

Mediterranean Landscape Design: Vernacular Contemporary
copyright © 2012 Thames & Hudson Ltd, London

Text copyright © 2012 Louisa Jones

Photographs unless otherwise credited copyright © 2012
Clive Nichols

Designed by Karolina Prymaka

All Rights Reserved. No part of this publication may be
reproduced or transmitted in any form or by any means,
electronic or mechanical, including photocopy, recording
or any other information storage and retrieval system,
without prior permission in writing from the publisher.

British Library Cataloguing-in-Publication Data
A catalogue record for this book is available from
the British Library

ISBN 978-0-500-51611-9

Printed and bound in China by C&C Offset Printing Co Ltd

To find out about all our publications, please visit
www.thamesandhudson.com There you can subscribe to
our e-newsletter, browse or download our current catalogue,
and buy any titles that are in print.

INTRODUCTION 6
MEDITERRANEAN 10
VERNACULAR 13
LANDSCAPE ART AND DESIGN 16

1 MOUNTAINS 20
TIME RECYCLED Digne-les-Bains, Haute Provence |
Andy Goldsworthy and herman de vries 27
NATURAL HISTORY Sentier des Lauzes, Ardèche |
Domingo Cisneros and Gilles Clément 30

2 STONEWORKS 34
QUARRY Strongilo and Kanonas, Corfu |
Rothschild family and Mary Keen 39
HILLSIDE TERRACING Fleur de l'Air, Provence |
Ian Hamilton Finlay; Clos Pascal and La Louve,
Provence | Nicole de Vésian 44

3 EARTHWORKS 54
PIGMENTS Bibémus, Provence | Philippe Deliau,
ALEP Agency 58
RAMMED EARTH Al Hossoun, Southern Morocco |
Arnaud Maurières and Eric Ossart 62

4 WOODWORKS 70
GLADE AND GROVE Fleur de l'Air, Provence |
Ian Hamilton Finlay; The Grove, French Riviera |
Jacqueline Morabito 74
TREES Mas de Michel, Le Terrain and La Carmejane, Provence |
Marc Nucera 80

5 CLIPPED GREENERY 86
TAPESTRIES La Louve, Provence | Nicole de Vésian 94
BLACK AND WHITE The Hamlet and The Grove,
French Riviera | Jacqueline Morabito 98

6 MATORRAL, MAQUIS, MEADOW 104

AEGEAN *PHRYGANA* OLIAROS, Antiparos, Greece |
doxiadis+ 108

TUSCAN *MACCHIA* Argentario, Tuscany |
Paolo Pejrone 114

MEADOW AND MATORRAL Mèze, Languedoc |
Olivier and Clara Filippi 120

7 FIELD GEOMETRIES 124

CLASSICAL CLARITY Sa Vina Vella, Mallorca |
Fernando Caruncho 131

SOFT MINIMALISM Mas de Benoît, Provence |
Alain David Idoux 136

8 GARDEN 142

ANGLO-ITALIAN Ninfa, Lazio | Caetani family 146

DESIGNER ITALIAN Bramafam, Piedmont |
Paolo Pejrone 152

MEDITERRANEAN HOME STYLE
La Malherbe, French Riviera | Mireille Ferrari 156

9 SEASCAPES 162

PLANETARY VISION Domaine du Rayol, French Riviera |
Gilles Clément 168

MEDITERRANEAN JAPANESE Peninsula Garden, Corsica |
Erik Borja 176

10 EMPORIUM 182

MASKS The Gardens of Venice I 186

COSMOPOLITAN VERNACULAR The Gardens of Venice II 192

11 MESURA 196

ROMANTIC CONTRADICTIONS Ninfa, Lazio |
Caetani family 200

ARCADIA IN MALLORCA Ariant, Mallorca |
Heidi Gildemeister 204

NOTES 214
BIBLIOGRAPHY 217
LIST OF ADDRESSES 219
ACKNOWLEDGMENTS 221
INDEX 222

INTRODUCTION

Human beings have been making land-scape art in the Mediterranean for some thirty thousand years.[2] Works of the imagination were then, as now, essential to continuing human life. The Italian tree sculptor Giuseppe Penone once noted a piece of graffiti that read 'Help! I'm disappearing!' and claimed that this cry is the motivation for all human action, especially art.[3] Never more so, perhaps, than today. Artists now working with Mediterranean landscapes are fascinated not by 'wilderness' or 'decadence' but by millennia of human negotiations with the land. Anyone sinking a spade or a post into Mediterranean soil today, building a dry-stone wall or pruning a tree, may ponder the layers of experience that have led to this place, this act, this skill. Moreover, the region's history of violent conflicts and intense trading since earliest times has by no means diminished its remarkable diversity, both cultural and biological.

The air is full of life, the earth of history.

Gilbert Highet, classical scholar, *Poets in a Landscape*, 1957[1]

A team of Franco-American scientists led by the French research scientist Jacques Blondel recently published an excellent study, *The Mediterranean Basin: Biological Diversity in Space and Time*. They claim that 'nowhere else but the Mediterranean has nature moulded people so much and people have in turn influenced nature. Human pressures on Mediterranean ecosystems have existed for so long that human activity should be considered as an integral ecological feature of the Mediterranean.' The great surprise is that this humanization of natural landscapes has been, on the whole, generative of life rather than destructive: 'There is often more biodiversity in

BELOW Mountains tumbling into the sea: a typical Mediterranean configuration, seen here on the northeast coast of Corfu, looking across to Albania.

OPPOSITE Remote, once poor coastal regions, like this part of Corfu, today attract cosmopolitan residents. Ancient vernacular skills now serve contemporary design projects that sometimes protect local landscapes, and sometimes endanger them.

a single square kilometre in the Mediterranean than in any area 100 times larger in the northern parts of Europe.'[4] Neither the climate zone, between temperate and tropical, nor the complex geological history of the region suffices to explain this. At a time when we are encouraged to 'tread lightly' on the earth, we learn with some amazement that these millennia of human meddling, in spite of numerous disasters past and present, have not been all bad.

The Mediterranean experience poses the urgent question: what is the role of human beings in nature? What powers do we possess, creative or harmful, and how are we using them? Is human enterprise 'cultural' and 'artificial', and therefore outside of – even opposed to – nature, as centuries of Western heritage would have us believe? Artists, as always, explore the frontiers. Today, landscape architects, designers, land artists, sculptors, gardeners and even poets are taking inspiration from age-old vernacular materials, skills and sites to produce landscape art that celebrates layers of living in this multifaceted region. Each work chosen for this book links ancient Mediterranean experience to a wider questioning about human beings and natural order. Each involves a strongly graphic vision on the scale of a whole landscape; each is site-generated (not transportable); each observes the logic of place as determined by local climate, geology, flora and fauna, architecture and land use; each is dynamic, insofar as vital process, growth, change and time are part of the creation.

The main terms used here – 'Mediterranean', 'vernacular', 'landscape art' and 'landscape design' – have all been variously defined by specialists, sometimes in contradiction with each other. The following clarifications should help, at the outset, to make them tools rather than problems.

ABOVE The Mediterranean climate zone is commonly defined by the distribution of one species of tree – the olive, lemon or orange. Experts apply more complex criteria. Courtyards like the one seen above in Mallorca also create sheltered microclimates.

OPPOSITE Wetlands and deltas, where rivers meet the sea and fresh water encounters salt, are as typically Mediterranean as dry scrubland. Seen here, the Bavella area of southern Corsica at sunrise.

MEDITERRANEAN

The Mediterranean is much more than a climate zone situated between tropical and temperate regions with long, dry summers and mild, wet winters. The pioneer French historian Fernand Braudel wrote half a century ago that the Mediterranean is 'one thousand things at a time. Not just one landscape but innumerable landscapes. Not just one sea, but a succession of seas. Not just one civilization but many civilizations packed on top of one another.'[5] Since the year 2000, several important books have extended Braudel's explorations towards defining 'a distinctively Mediterranean sense of place', stressing 'the interactions between humanity and the changing set of environmental conditions'.[6] The conclusions of scientists and historians converge in ways that are often provocative. Both the region's distinctiveness and its rich diversity result, firstly, from the sea itself and the opportunities it has always offered for exchange and discovery, and secondly, from a unique geological history that has produced a dense and small-scaled 'mosaic of habitats and an astonishing heterogeneity of local topographies, soil types and microclimates'.[7] As succinctly defined by the poet W. H. Auden, the Mediterranean is a region of 'short distances and definite places'.[8]

Defining the limits of the Mediterranean is not easy. Often the distribution area of a single species, the olive tree or holm oak, serves as a guide. The biodiversity experts meticulously demonstrate the limits of this approach and opt for more complex 'bioclimatic' standards. The area they outline includes in fact 'a dozen majestic mountain ranges, a kaleidoscope of forests, woodlands and shrublands, a host of riparian, coastal and other wetlands and the sea itself, with its archipelago of many thousands of islands'. They conclude that, with its 'eight main cultural and linguistic groups' and three major religions, the Mediterranean is 'a socio-ecological mosaic like no other in the world'.[9]

Today's wave of interest in the Mediterranean runs counter to an earlier Romantic vision, one which has enchanted northern travellers, poets and painters for the last two centuries. Decadence was long the keynote. Accumulated layers of experience were equated with ruins

LEFT AND ABOVE Mediterranean regions show wide variations in soil, stone, topography and crops. Squashes, like tomatoes, introduced from the Americas centuries ago, come in many regional varieties today because of differing climates and soil.

as economic and political power shifted elsewhere. Neglected or impoverished landscapes became poignant reminders of mortality. Scientists and historians might deplore rather than enjoy them, but the sense of decay was the same. This is what the distinguished conservationist and landscape historian Oliver Rackham calls the 'irreversible ruin' theory: he attributes it to 'historians from Northern Europe or influenced by north and central European thought habits'.[10] Jacques Blondel and his team agree with this judgment and claim, moreover, that 'although there is no doubt that large-scale destruction has taken place and that much of the shrublands in the Mediterranean are modified or derived – not to say degraded – forms of former forests and woodlands, it is indisputable that the exceptional diversity and dynamic structure of Mediterranean ecosystems and communities result in part from human influence'.[11] The

ABOVE Winds on the Aegean island of Antiparos assail both author Louisa Jones and a native juniper. These trees, called 'snake trees' locally because of their wind-twisted silhouettes, are rare today because their wood was much exported during the seventeenth century.

British historians Peregrine Horden and Nicholas Purcell, working independently, arrive at similar conclusions. Quite a flurry arose in the year 2000 when they published their monumental history of the Mediterranean, taking a stand against the 'Romantic, progressivist and evolutionist parti-pris' of accounts 'linking cultural complexity to technical progress and the rise of northern European capitalism, treating prehistory and antiquity as mere forerunners'.[12] Their work gave rise to a colloquium and collection of critical essays, *Rethinking the Mediterranean*. All these scholars challenge the Romantic vision, worthy of study as a cultural phenomenon in its own right but misleading, insofar as Romantics, often quite deliberately, value imagination and emotion over observation and discovery.

The Romantic heritage persists with some force today in ecological movements that oppose pure nature to corrupt humankind. Examples of both persuasions – the veneration of nature without man and a humanist ecology that accepts our presence – can be found in these pages. However, most of the artists present value the Mediterranean not because of the old sirens of primitivism, decadence and decay, but because it allows them to explore the human presence in nature as symbiosis rather than conflict.

VERNACULAR

Mediterranean diversity has always been closely connected to 'vernacular' traditions and practices. The architecture historian Victor Papanek, a strong advocate of ecologically responsible design, examined vernacular examples worldwide in order to provide specific criteria: 'If we look up the word "vernacular" in a dictionary, we find definitions such as anonymous, indigenous, naïve, naïf, primitive, rude, popular, spontaneous, local or folk-based.'[13] He warns against six common fallacies in the usage of this term: the historic (being old is not enough); the exotic (being far away is not enough); the romantic (Arcadian idealism or the 'noble savage' fantasy); the popular (fast food joints do not qualify); the 'living tradition' (shopping malls do not qualify) and the sacred (cathedrals do not qualify). He offers himself a rich summary that suits the Mediterranean version very well: 'Vernacular architecture is based on a knowledge of traditional practices and techniques; it is usually self-built (perhaps with help from family, clan or builders in the tribe), and reveals a

OPPOSITE This idyllic olive grove in Corfu looks natural but belongs to a garden designed by the Skopos agency. Have the rounded clumps been shaped by wind, by grazing or by the gardener's hand?

BELOW Grazing animals like this happy billy goat near Campo in Mallorca are part of a management strategy for sustainable land use going back to prehistoric times.

high regard for craftsmanship and quality. Vernacular structures tend to be easy to learn and understand. They are made of predominantly local materials. They are ecologically apt, that is they fit in well with local climate, flora, fauna, ways of life. Vernacular buildings are never self-conscious; they recede into the environment rather than serving as self-proclaiming design statements. They are human in scale; frequently the process of building is more important than or equally important as the end product. This combination of good ecological fit, human scale, craftsmanship and striving for quality, together with a strong concern for decoration, ornamentation and embellishment, leads to sensual frugality that results in true elegance.'[14]

The vernacular is often associated with 'peasantry', another highly charged term. Here, too, the British historians Horden and Purcell challenge common assumptions and claim that human beings who survive by adapting to the 'unpredictable, the variable and above all the local' must display 'a degree of agility and adaptability which does not fit the usual definitions of peasantry.'[15] Peasant conservatism, they demonstrate, has often been a way of rejecting colonialism posing as progress, technologies that render locals dependent on outside networks. Peasants are often acknowledged in France today as the first 'landscape architects',[16] but sometimes with the condescending assumption that they were not aiming at beauty as such and were oblivious to the harmonies they achieved.[17] There exist, however, numerous testimonials to aesthetic awareness in peasant communities. Provençal writer Jean Giono wrote about remote mountain villagers in the early 1950s: 'Pruning predisposes to reverie and satisfies at small expense the creative urge... Add to that the fact that a well-pruned tree is a source of pride, and if it is near a path or in the hills where people walk on Sundays, if it is really well done, they will come to see it as if it were a show!'[18] This is still true today in many places.

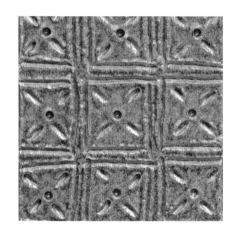

THIS PAGE AND OPPOSITE ABOVE AND BELOW A detail of a ceramic plate; textured walls, roof tiles and pots in Mallorca; a craftsman at the Europa Impruneta factory in Tuscany. Vernacular art uses local materials and skills to create objects that are both beautiful and useful. These require an eye and imagination; head as well as hand.

ABOVE AND CENTRE RIGHT A row of glass jugs on a table in a Mallorcan hotel; a detail of wrought-iron furniture, designed by the American Garrett Finney, who often takes inspiration from vernacular art, for Judy Pillsbury at La Louve in Provence, former home of the legendary Nicole de Vésian.

LANDSCAPE ART AND DESIGN

Gilles Tiberghien, one of the best-known contemporary experts on land and nature art,[19] endorses the view that 'we must learn to respect the traditional approaches of the sailor and the peasant'.[20] In several books, this historian traces the work of American Land Artists of the 1960s,[21] quite resolutely Romantic in their rejection of consumerist society, their fascination with the energies of decay and their withdrawal into 'wilderness'. Their retreats were, however, nuclear testing grounds in deserts and salt lakes, sites they often strenuously restructured to provide settings for their individual gestures. Robert Smithson's *Spiral Jetty* is an iconic example.[22] Later on, European nature and environmental art still mainly regarded sites as pretexts but were nonetheless often inspired by local spirit of place. Growth and fertility remained excluded from this essentially nomadic art,

BELOW Hillside terracing, seen here at the Sentier des Lauzes site in southern France, is a form of landscape sculpture that dates back to the Bronze Age.

however, partly because, as the German historian Udo Weilacher puts it, 'the living plant often develops an unpredictable momentum of its own and actively alters its environment'. Weilacher concludes: 'When working with nature, the artist is forced to enter into a dialogue with the independent existence of his subject matter or, at least, to come to terms with it.'[23]

In fact, many 'nature' artists today still strenuously avoid any such 'dialogue with the independent existence of [their] subject matter'. The pathetic fallacy dear to the Romantics – the imaginative projection of the artist's personality onto nature, ostensibly worshipped but in fact serving mainly as a stimulus for self-exploration – is very much alive in our time. The vocabulary has cooled down: instead of emotion and imagination, artists experiment with 'concept' and 'perception', but the process is still essentially anthropomorphic. Photography can pose further screens between an artist and recognition of any Other. The spectator is at an even greater distance. Often lost along the way today are direct sensuous experience and pleasure. Mediterranean regions can offer a good deal of both, and many of the artists they attract find growth is as compelling as decay. They are full of wonder at the discovery of something beyond the Self, even though, as the French gardener-artist Gilles Clément says: 'When we work with life, we determine only the starting point.'[24]

For many Romantics, the local merely serves as a launching pad to jump from the personal to the universal. This often deliberate uprooting corresponded in the 1960s to a similar urge among modernist architects wishing to escape any suspicion of regionalism. Today, much landscape art worldwide is, on the contrary, fascinated with 'spirit of place' to the point of being not just 'site-specific' but 'site-generated'. Tiberghien recently wrote about the contemporary sculptor James Turrell's Roden Crater in the Arizona desert: 'I like artists who offer a genuine aesthetic experience of space, light and nature. Their propositions concern particular perceptions

ABOVE Greek hillside terracing redesigned by the doxiadis+ agency. This and the French example (opposite) are both graphically defined and small-scaled, and meet similar needs with similar techniques; they illustrate what ethnologist Claude Lévi-Strauss called 'those differences that resemble each other'.

of space but at the same time offer a whole world view.' He goes on to reflect that gardens, even the most conventional, have always embodied just such an experience...[25]

Can gardens be legitimately treated as part of landscape art? A critic of a previous generation lamented that 'much of the great creative potential of landscape design has been dissipated by a preoccupation with the private, the decorative and the ephemeral'.[26] How does current Mediterranean landscape art deal with these presumed limitations? To start with the ephemeral: weather – particularly local, erratic and violent in the Mediterranean – is as crucial for landscape artists as it is for peasants and sailors. Artists link instants and eons, the momentary and the ancient, art and geology. And where growth becomes part of an artwork, the moment is both unpredictable and part of a long continuity with its own logic. Secondly, the word 'decorative' is very ambiguous in a Mediterranean context. Peasant cultures are sometimes deemed pure of the 'merely decorative' because it is assumed that subsistence living must be solely functional. The beauty of vernacular buildings, tools and landscapes is attributed to an essential equation between gesture and use, an ideal appealing to lovers of austere 'minimalism'. An opposing point of view dismisses both the functional and the decorative as equally domestic, too humble for 'pure' art. But Mediterranean cultures have never separated use from beauty, nor 'handicraft' from 'high' art, the mundane from the sublime. Odysseus admired fine bed linens and knew exactly how to make a raft. Peasant communities have constantly supplied both basic and luxury markets with pottery, fabrics, carpets, wood and metalwork (see pp. 14–15), including jewelry. Does this make vernacular art (or craft) 'merely' decorative? How should music be classified in these spurious hierarchies?

As for 'the preoccupation with the private', there, too, the Romantic and the Mediterranean require different approaches. Tiberghien points out that those who consider art mainly as provocation cannot accept an 'amiable', much less a community vision.[27]

BELOW Industrial agriculture – here, lavender fields in Provence – imposes photogenic geometries on land forms, but works against natural balance. The mechanical harvesting of such a field kills thousands of bees.

The Romantic artist is the most private of all: he stands alone, outside and against society. In traditional Mediterranean cultures, wilderness and solitude have had little appeal. Artists and poets are not outcasts but heroes, even folk heroes. The British writer Lawrence Durrell noted admiringly: 'The Mediterranean has always been full of poets and every village in Cyprus has at least two. It is a communal gift rather than a personal one.'[28] Both Greek and Roman societies considered gardens, like agronomy, to be fit subjects for great poets.

Outdated classifications exist also in garden history. The eminent scholar John Dixon Hunt, founder of the journal *Studies in the History of Gardens and Designed Landscapes*, concludes when describing the gardens of Venice: 'Both the distinction ritualistically invoked by all garden historians between "formal" and "informal" gardening and the teleology that guides the narrative of "progress" from an autocratic and geometrical to a "natural", "unconstrained" and "free" style are even more than usually irrelevant to Venice... Conventional terminology and teleology seem useless, labels like baroque or picturesque so often serve as blinkers not magnifying glasses.'[29] Venetian gardens, for various reasons which he himself explores, have quite simply kept the vernacular profile characteristic of Mediterranean gardens generally (see pp. 180–95).

Is vernacular inspiration for contemporary art today just a new form of pastoral idealism? For Horden and Purcell, 'the view that humans have had almost entirely negative impacts on nature – widespread among environmental historians, historical geographers, ecologists and environmentalists – paradoxically perpetuates the old Western stereotypes of humanity as active, dominating, and separate from a nature that is passive and static. A view more in tune with late twentieth-century empirical data and current ecological theory would emphasize that relationships between humans and nature are interactive and embedded within a kaleidoscopic environment in which little or nothing is permanent.'[30]

John Dixon Hunt once wrote that 'Land Art seems to restore to landscape architecture its old and largely lost concern for the intricate melding of site, sight and insight'.[31] Landscape design today follows this example, but with deeper regard for the specifics of place, especially in the Mediterranean, where, still, 'the air is full of life, the earth of history'.

MOUNTAINS

... adjusted to the local needs of valleys

Where everything can be touched or reached by walking.

W. H. Auden, 'In Praise of Limestone', 1948[1]

'Mountains come first,' wrote Fernand Braudel. 'The familiar landscapes of vines and olive trees and urbanized villages are merely the fringe.'[1] Mediterranean mountains have sheltered gods and goddesses, saints, witches and hermits, shrines and sanctuaries, since earliest human history. They constitute barriers but also passages – for shepherds, pilgrims, heretics and resistance fighters and, once, for Hannibal's elephants. Mountain peoples, free from the diseases and raids that beset coastal populations, defy outside governance: some, as brigands, prey on lowland travellers. Mountains supply most of the Mediterranean's minerals and seasonal labour forces for the plains. Certain cash crops need mountain conditions – lavender succeeds best when grown above 1,000 metres in altitude. Snow, lasting into summer on peaks, was for centuries a mountain export that allowed the Italians to invent ice cream. Jean Giono described tough mountain settlements in Provence, remembering villagers who loved 'these landscapes that are nine-tenths sky and one-tenth earth, earth you look down on, visions that can make a soul delirious with joy'.[2]

However lyrical, this is not a vision of Romantic solitude. Such high-perched communities were once well populated, linked by paths from summit to summit. Most declined steadily after World War II. Art trails for hikers represent one clever way of creating new economic resources from this vernacular heritage while adding a new layer of human experience to the places thus revived. The Geological Reserve of

PAGE 20 The buckling of the Provence Alps reveals in places strata from several eras all at once, still evolving imperceptibly. Andy Goldsworthy's Art Refuge at the Vieil Esclangon sits opposite.

BELOW The River Bès at Digne-les-Bains, Haute Provence. Andy Goldsworthy wrote about it: 'The river is a very strong expression of flow and connection and movement and I would like to feel that I can find the river in a tree, in a stone.'

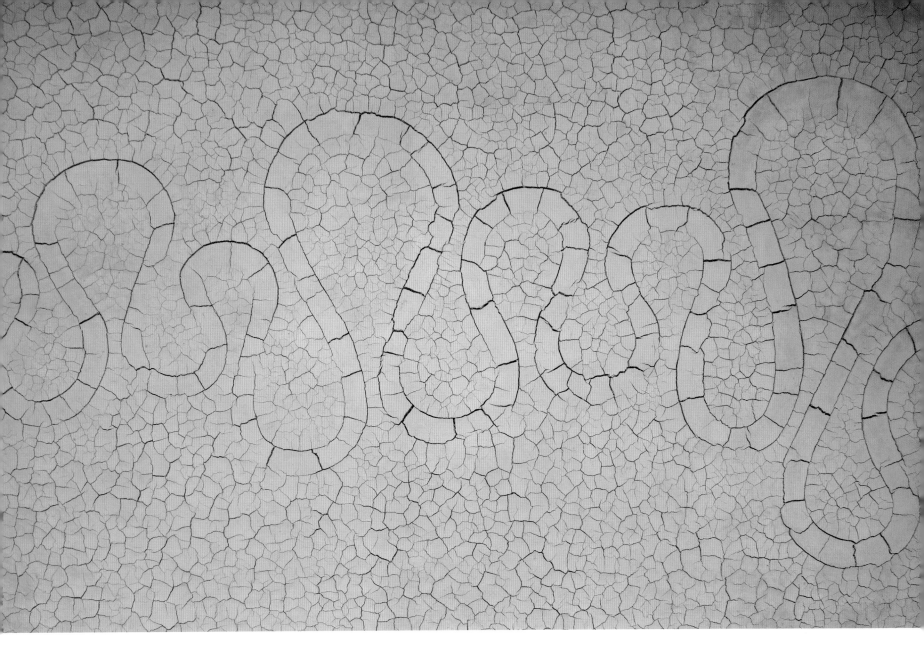

the Alpes de Haute Provence was founded as a private association in 1985 around Digne-les-Bains, a spa town in the Provence Alps, where several river valleys converge at the foot of mountains. Digne also marks the limit of olive tree hardiness. The Reserve now spreads over fifty-nine townships, covers some 2,300 square kilometres and is part of the Global Geoparks network supported by UNESCO. One of its founders was Nadine Gomez, who first trained as a geologist, then as a museum curator. In 1995, for the birthday celebration of the Reserve, Gomez invited the British artist Andy Goldsworthy to work at Digne on the theme of 'earth and life'. He has been returning regularly ever since. He recalls: 'The Alpes de Haute Provence department was wondering how to revive a deserted countryside. The idea of combining long-distance walking with artworks took root. I adore working in agricultural settings so I came

ABOVE Andy Goldsworthy's famous clay wall, 'River of Earth', was commissioned by curator Nadine Gomez for the town museum at Digne-les-Bains in Haute Provence. There are more of Goldsworthy's works grouped in this region than anywhere else in the world.

up with the idea of new uses for ruined buildings.'[3] Thus began the Art Refuges, six restored buildings and three cairns so far, spread out in a wide circle that links crests and valleys. Asked today why he keeps coming to Digne, the artist says that it is because of the people – Nadine Gomez, but also Jean-Pierre Brovelli, a 'cultural' mountain guide, and Eric Klein, an architect who helps the artist with the restoration work. Brovelli brings small groups from all over the world to 'do the walk', for three to six days, a life-changing experience for many of them. He and Gomez maintain the refuges and trails with their own hands.

Gomez reorganized the modest town museum of Digne around a powerful dialogue between art and natural science – the kind based on direct, outdoor observation. She took as her motto '*Ambulo, ergo sum*' (I walk, therefore I am), a phrase coined by Pierre Gassendi, a seventeenth-century celebrity of Digne. Gassendi was a theologian, astronomer, philosopher and naturalist, who exchanged views with Descartes, Galileo, Kepler and Hobbes. In 1885, the museum was first founded and named after Gassendi by another impressive local son, Etienne Martin, scientist, naturalist, scholar and landscape painter. Today, in collaboration with the Reserve, it sponsors artists-in-residence with a view to exhibits, permanent works and publications. It also houses Goldsworthy's famous clay wall, *River of Earth*, and works by Dutch artist herman de vries, a regular participant since 1999. For de vries, as for Goldsworthy, nature is not merely a setting, nor even a subject to be depicted, but *la chose même*, the thing itself.[4] Both have generously donated their outdoor works, scattered

ABOVE AND RIGHT The Vieil Esclangon, Haute Provence. Hikers can spend the night in this restored barn, watching firelight play on the intimate serpentine constructed by Andy Goldsworthy. The sculpture is made from red clay, like the soil of the winding path up to the pass.

along the mountain trails, to the museum. Recently, Gomez was designated art director for a trail covering 190 kilometres and linking Provence and Piedmont, baptised VIAPAC (*Via per l'arte contemporanea*, see also p. 210). Hiking herself, she scouts out sites with strong character to tempt artists who work in original ways with nature. Currently listed are Mark Dion, Jean-Luc Vilmouth, Paul-Armand Gette, Stéphane Bérard, Joan Fontcuberta, David Renaud and Richard Nonas. The latter, trained as an anthropologist, began work at the abandoned village of Vière, near Digne. He was moved by the site's rich past to the point of suggesting that this 'life in which close-to-the-bone, barely sustainable survival in just-barely-supportive mountains is still the definition of what life should be'.[5]

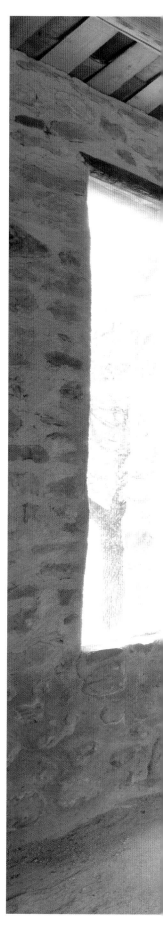

TIME RECYCLED

Andy Goldsworthy wrote in 1999 that the Art Refuge project 'fits extremely well into my own need for having a strong and deep relationship with particular places'. At the same time, Digne has allowed him to experiment with new forms, materials and textures that then become part of his works elsewhere. Many of his first efforts were ephemeral, for example, woven leaf arrangements floating in a river bed in the heart of a storm. He has developed an uncanny ability to sense very local conditions, even weather patterns, wherever he works.[6] Few places have as much variability as Digne, both meteorological and geological. The buckling of the Alps has in places created deep gorges revealing strata from several eras all at once. One of the Art Refuges, a ruined farmhouse on the terraced site of the former village of Vieil Esclangon, overlooks this amazing spectacle – still shifting, observes the mountain guide, Jean-Pierre Brovelli. Cows graze the meadows among the globe thistles and Alpine sea holly, Spanish broom and wild roses. Inside the house is a serpentine wall sculpture by Goldsworthy made from local red clay. It is almost entirely enclosed but subtly lit by a side window, by the fireplace opposite and sometimes, for those who stay here overnight, by moonlight. Goldsworthy pays meticulous attention not only to materials and textures but also to light, shifting according to weather, time of day and season.

An hour away on foot is the restored barn of the Col de l'Escuichière, where the soil is marly limestone rather than the more acid sandstone. Here a copse of shady beech trees is surrounded by wild thyme and lavender. Goldsworthy was originally inspired here by the remains of charcoal burning, an important vernacular resource, but then he noticed lines of pure white calcite in the dark stone of a ruined barn. Observing that the original builders had already made playful patterns with this striking variation, he was moved to follow their example on inside walls, where the lines will not weather and fade. This work, he says, 'grew up from the place like the house itself'. So, in a sense, has the whole Art Refuge project. It has never been

Digne-les-Bains, Haute Provence | Andy Goldsworthy
The artist assembles natural lines of white calcite in dark limestone. He considers his sculpture at Col de l'Escuichière to be 'a line of energy, movement and flow', like a river.

conceived as an overall plan but evolved, says the artist, 'organically, like vernacular architecture' (partly due to financing as unpredictable as weather!). Goldsworthy considers that the Art Refuges constitute his most important work, but one that, in a sense, will never be finished.[7]

He explains: 'I work in a landscape made rich by the people who have worked and farmed in it. I can feel the presence of those who have gone before me. This puts my own life into context. My touch is the most recent of many layers that are embedded in the landscape, which in turn will be covered by future layers…' Like the farmers and craftsmen before him, Goldworthy feels: 'It is the way of nature to be used, worked and touched. All of nature here has been touched.' He adds, 'I am not interested in categorizing nature; the scientific approach. I have the countryman's basic general knowledge of it.' Goldsworthy's Art Refuges involved numerous meetings with rural populations whose background is very similar to his own. Engaging their participation was one of the team's major aims.

Herman de vries has a quite different approach. At the Vieil Esclangon site, for example, he has etched, then outlined in gold leaf, a discreet infinity sign on a small rock. Neither the symbol nor the materials are site-specific. At La Roche-Rousse, the artist created a 'Nature Sanctuary' around an abandoned farmhouse, below a fourteenth-century chapel. Notwithstanding their presence, the artist writes about 'unspoilt' nature, a 'garden without a gardener'. Human experience is acknowledged by the addition of a Sanskrit inscription (more global than local), intended to express 'a form of respect, almost religious, for the natural world'.[8] When de vries embraces a six-hundred-year-old oak or runs naked through the forest, it is the artist's own gesture that signifies and is recorded by accompanying journalists. Neither the tree nor the site merits attention. The creative act joins the personal to the universal without involving any local specifics. The British artist Antony Gormley takes a similar stance in the Austrian Alps with *Horizon Field*: one hundred giant cast-iron statues of his own nude body scattered over 150 square kilometres of high mountain slopes. Like de vries, Gormley gives primacy to 'personal experience', all the more valued for being far from 'the mediated world of human habitations'.[9] He chooses to ignore the fact that these mountains, too, have long been populated, even depicted on postcards. Just the authorizations from landowners for this project must have involved highly complex negotiations. Media and visitor attention remains focused on the statues, not their setting, still less the relationship between the two.

Digne-les-Bains, Haute Provence | herman de vries

In his series 'Traces', de vries has placed symbols and words
in nine languages over an area of two square kilometres –
a game of hide and seek for art-loving hikers.

NATURAL HISTORY

Gilles Clément, designer, ecologist and writer, was trained both as an agronomist and landscape architect. His public works are acclaimed worldwide, among them the Parc Citroën and Musée Branly gardens in Paris and the Domaine du Rayol in the south of France (see pp. 168–75). Clément has long been wary of Art. He prefers people to Humanity and ecosystems to Nature. He first drew notice in the 1980s as advocate of the 'moving garden', an exploration of the flux of evolving, abandoned farmland. Far from admiring 'gardens without gardeners', he insists on the importance of human beings in the biosphere. His ideal is not 'unspoilt' wilderness, real or imaginary, but a 'planetary garden': he calls on humans to act as gardeners in their careful nurturing of the globe as a whole. Recently, he has encouraged the protection of 'landscapes of the third kind', spaces presently unused by human beings that become a refuge for biodiversity. He might have written, like Goldsworthy, 'I am part of nature, I don't see myself as being in opposition, and I see it as a strange idea to see us as separate from nature. Our lives and what we do affect nature so closely that we cannot be separate from it.'

Clément has become an artist in spite of himself in the context of a French 'art and landscape discovery trail'[10] called the 'Sentier des Lauzes'. Such was the name adopted by a non-profit association founded in 2000, a mix of locals and incomers. Architect-urbanist Martin Chénot, a founder, describes this rugged and breathtaking part of the south-central French massif as 'one of those abandoned terraced landscapes in the Mediterranean with an uncertain future'. Here, too, the aim is to protect and renew both natural beauty and rural economy by establishing a project with an international reputation. The picturesque valley of the Drobie thus becomes a 'cultural valley', offering hikers a circuit of some five hours designed to reveal artworks using local materials – stone (the slate slabs locally called 'lauzes'), water, vegetation, wind, weather. The series began in 2001 with a work by Mexican artist Domingo Cisneros called 'Parole de Lauzes'.

Clément has helped this community understand that the valley's reforestation reveals a natural dynamic rather than a kind of deterioration.

Sentier des Lauzes, Ardèche | Domingo Cisneros
The Mexican artist Domingo Cisneros inaugurated this mountain art trail in 2001 with 'Parole de Lauzes', twenty shale figures inspired by traditional ridgepoles. Above: 'The Spirit of the Mountain'. Opposite: 'The Family'.

The Association now uses its considerable energies to make 'clearings' of several kinds, including the art trail, which it protects from landscape closure as from the invasive wild boar. The woods of pines, chestnut and evergreen oaks, and the scrublands of heather and broom, are now valued as landscapes of the third kind in various stages of evolution. Each clearing also participates in the network of planetary gardens – not an abstract universal but a fabric woven globally by hands-on human effort.

Clément was invited to add a work of his own to the trail, the *Belvédère des lichens* ('Lichen Belvedere'). The structures themselves are unobtrusive: simple wooden platforms placed among lichen-covered rocks allow an appreciation of both detail and distance. The eye moves from the subtle patterning of the lichens to the contours of the rocks and out towards the medieval chapel of Saint-Régis and the perched village of Dompnac. Outlines, textures and tones participate in the same sense of flow. But Clément is a naturalist, concerned not only to feel but to know. It matters very much to him that lichens are a symbiotic union of algae and mushrooms, and that these four species – pale *Rhizocarpon*, silvery *Parmelia*, stiff sombre *Lasallia* and grey *Aspicilia* – involve different scales not only in space but also in time. In addition, some species indicate clean air. Learning how they live gives wider resonances to the art without the abstraction of symbol. This particular mix can only exist right here, at this moment, and will already be different tomorrow.

All the mountain art trails ask Antony Gormley's question: 'What is the place of humans in the order of things?'[11] Romantic veneration comes easily in such sites, where people seem so very small. But the art trails are about communities and communication as well as creation. Language, like photography, may intensify or dilute private emotion. Goldsworthy refuses on-site labelling but counts on local mountain guides as well as his own publications. For de vries, the works themselves are often inscriptions in ancient languages, usually unintelligible to visitors whom in any case he refuses to inform, saying that the important thing is to look, not to find. Paul-Armand Gette, a prolific writer, is planning elaborate word plays for his new work in Digne. Gilles Clément plans an orientation table giving exact information on the lichens. Each artist's preferences are respected by the organizers. As Nadine Gomez says, these are all projects 'full of intelligence and passion; there is no question of turning them into products'. The important thing, writes Martin Chénot, is to keep walking, to 'harvest the landscape' with eyes, muscles, feet, mind and dreams.

Sentier des Lauzes, Ardèche | Gilles Clément
The 'Lichen Belvedere', an installation by naturalist Gilles Clément, draws attention not to itself but to the setting, from the lichens that colour the stone to the distant prospect, connecting close exploration to far horizons.

STONEWORKS

Men always pick up a stone when they are afraid.

They stick it in a field – it becomes a dolmen.

They put it in a desert – it becomes an obelisk.

Ways of measuring mystery and time, what a consolation!

Jean Giono, *La Pierre*, 1955[1]

The Mediterranean, say Jacques Blondel and his team of biodiversity experts, 'is one of the most geologically complex areas in the world and the only case of a large sea surrounded by three continents'.[2] As with climate and vegetation, the rock and stone of this region are subject to huge local variability over short distances. The extraction, improving and trading of minerals have been going on since earliest times, especially in the Aegean. Even the characteristic Mediterranean limestone differs in the amount and size of its quartz and organic debris, hardness, porosity, ease of work and capacity to harden once exposed to the air. Deep within it hide grottoes and underground rivers in constant evolution. Stone goes with water in Mediterranean landscapes as yin goes with yang. Mediterranean folklore often features fearsome dragons surging forth on the site of powerful springs. Erosion control and irrigation were long the major motivations for shaping and sculpting the land.

PAGE 34 The limestone of northeastern Corfu in a rough outcrop, a drystone wall and flat paving, intermingled at the Rou Estate (architect Dom Skinner).

ABOVE AND OPPOSITE Vernacular drystone construction requires considerable skill and defines many Mediterranean landscapes. A wall in southern Mallorca (above); a shepherd's hut at Trabari in Provence (opposite), now part of the landscape art of Nicole de Vésian.

QUARRY

Caves and grottoes, as Homer and Dante illustrate, allow humans to communicate with tectonic powers. Quarries provide less dramatic but more graphic links to the underworld, bearing witness not only to the force of natural energies but also to human effort through time. Vernacular builders needed very local quarries: in the 1970s, more than one hundred were inventoried in the French department of the Vaucluse alone. Many former quarries have been converted into display spaces by artists, as in the gardens of César Manrique in the Canary Islands or the Hortus Unicorni by Elio Cavallo and Luca De Troia in Etruria. Elsewhere (in Malta, for example) quarries now offer protected sites for specialized market gardening.

The Greek island of Corfu has whole forests of lofty olive trees punctuated by wild cypress. Long occupation by the Venetian republic marked its traditional architecture with red and gold stucco, but the northeastern peninsulas were always too poor for such luxury. Farmhouses there were built from a particularly lovely limestone that ages well and has flecks that glint like gold. Today, no longer poor, this area is familiarly known as Kensington-on-Sea. Many of its properties sit on steep spurs jutting out into the sea, where a series of misty islands lead the eye towards Albania. Most have landscaped gardens, where natural rock outcrops blend with drystone constructions to make landscape art.

The gem of these gardens and surely the oldest is a Rothschild property, unique in its diversity and in the series of talented artists, including the owners, who have contributed to its evolution. Two headlands, Kanonas and Strongilo, circumscribe the site. Rough rock and stone recombine here in many subtle ways, bearing witness to history as much as to modern artistry. The British landscape designer and writer Mary Keen, advisor to the Rothschilds, considers that 'the light that beguiled so many painters, the glimpses of sea through olives and cypresses, the ancient boles of trees among rocks, the

OPPOSITE The quarry rockface of the Rou Estate in Corfu now shelters heat-loving agaves as well as swimmers in the nearby pool.

RIGHT Remains of a Roman settlement, once built with stone quarried on site, at the Prieuré Saint-Symphorien in Provence.

wildflowers in spring and autumn all proclaim this secret paradise beyond the skill of any gardener. Anything that has ever happened on Kanonas and Strongilo has been a reinforcement of what is there, an attempt to make the place more itself.'[3]

A Greek painter, Nicolas Ghika (1906–1994), first built the elegant residence with his wife Barbara, mother of the present owner, Lord Rothschild. The latter commissioned new buildings designed by Timothy Hatton Associates, collected classical statuary for the site and still oversees all of its metamorphoses. It was his idea to bare dramatic rock formations and to encourage small-scaled 'land art' assemblages on the lower drystone terraces. Mary Keen has advised on plantings throughout, mixing horticultural choices and existing vegetation with great discretion. She has

Strongilo, Corfu | Rothschild family and Mary Keen

The quarry pool with plantings by Beth Rothschild. The evergreen banks of rosemary and myrtle suggest waves, connecting pool to sea, while the olive trees frame the view towards Albania. Their opalescent foliage echoes the tones of paving and rockface. The pool establishes a general harmony between stone, water and vegetation, linking earth, sea and sky.

also laid paths in white limestone, beautifully judged curves and lines in strategic places leading down through the olive terraces of Kanonas, past an elegant citrus orchard and vegetable garden, and up to the heights of Strongilo. Keen says she likes to design 'narrow paths' that encounter 'things that make you duck and weave. You can't walk fast and you can't see what is ahead – this makes for mystery and surprise.'[4] A stone arch hides the entrance to the most breathtaking part of the gardens at the top of Strongilo: a former quarry transformed into a swimming pool by the Spanish architect Javier Barba.

A Rothschild daughter, Beth (trained as a gardener at Kew), added plantings to make the pool less visible from the sea – mature olive trees, as well as 'waves' of myrtle and rosemary, now regularly clipped by caretakers Andy and Karen Belton. Above the pool, more paths wind up through stony scrubland to the Grotto Garden, a smaller quarry site where spring rains have formed stalactites. The run-off from this space waters meadows further on, where, as Mary Keen relates, 'bulbs star the grass and the trees are pruned into airy shapes'. Another daughter, Emmy, the Beltons and Mary Keen herself used stones from the quarry to build here a cairn in 'Homage to Andy Goldsworthy'. At the top of the hill, a massive stone fortress rises from a broad terrace of local limestone slabs, offering the best sea views – yet another blending of stone and water, the idiom of this property.

The mixture of wild and garden plantings is well adapted to the long dry spells which affect all the different microclimates that even just one hillside can provide. Myrtle, lentisk, phlomis, euphorbia, bupleurum and rosemary have all been introduced here. But as Mary Keen concludes: 'For plant lovers, the greatest glory of the estate is the wild flowers. Cyclamen carpet the olive groves, tiny Narcissi and Corfiot snowdrops are out before Christmas. Orchids appear throughout the year, and in spring, cranesbills and pink Crepis are everywhere. The ancient, untouched, natural peace of the place is what counts most at Kanonas.'

Kanonas, Corfu | Rothschild family and Mary Keen
Between the original villa and the terraced olive orchard below, sparse topsoil was removed to reveal layers of natural rock. The path downhill is marked by landscape sculptures inseparable from the site.

HILLSIDE TERRACING

Drystone terracing has been called both a 'hallmark speciality' of Mediterranean landscapes[5] and one of 'the most significant living landscapes in the world'.[6] Farmers have fought erosion for millennia by creating these flat spaces for cultivation, using stones picked when clearing fields to build retaining walls and channel storm run-off into storage cisterns. The stonework looks solid, but, in a climate alternating drought and violent storms, where sheep and goats, wild boar and deer often roam, these are vulnerable sites requiring constant upkeep. It takes skill and experience to build durable terracing.

In ancient civilizations such as Mesopotamia and Egypt, terraces were part of complex irrigation systems built by slaves. In the European vernacular, they were built by individuals, families and communities. In 1924, American writer Alice Martineau advised cosmopolitan Riviera gardeners: 'The method of rough walling may be safely left to the peasants, who thoroughly understand it.'[7] William Graves describes living in Mallorca with his poet father, Robert, in 1946: 'Practically everyone owned a few terraces of olive trees and grew wheat on them... New terracing went on all the time – an art passed down from father to son.'[8] Drystone construction is undergoing a big revival in Europe today.

Unlike the formal structures of princely gardens, in which whole hillsides are regraded, vernacular terraces espouse the existing contours of the terrain. Slopes are divided into separate but linked spaces, each with its own character, shape and dimensions. Any symmetry is accidental. From within, these sites offer multiple viewpoints: their orchards, fields and vineyards can be seen from above, below and across, both diagonally and horizontally. Many terraced hillsides also have panoramic prospects outwards as well, which modern designers treat in different ways: some simply edit and frame the view with plantings, others use it like the backdrop of a stage, still others link near and far through a series of graded planes. There can also be a vantage point onto the site from the slope opposite, a sightline exploited in designed gardens by architects

ABOVE Medieval hilltowns such as Gordes in Provence were often built on rings of drystone terracing serving as ramparts and creating shaded cobblestone streets.

who used earthworks to impose formal symmetries. This is rarely the case with agricultural properties. All hillside terracing offers an exceptional mix of exposure and enclosure, while its strong graphic definition allows for much internal diversity.

Ian Hamilton Finlay, poet and gardener of the iconic Little Sparta in Scotland, worked with his associate Pia Simig to create the 'Fleur de l'Air' gardens on a terraced site in Provence. The owners had already restored the drystone walls supporting dozens of mature olive trees on this property. Like his eighteenth-century predecessor, 'Capability' Brown, Finlay claimed that, 'my particular talent is for making use of whatever possibility is there'.[9] He was quite aware of what his admirer and chronicler John Dixon Hunt calls 'the obvious virtues of vernacular gardening' and had already worked with vernacular settings, in '"found" olive plantations as in woodland groves'[10] (see p. 76). The hillside in Provence offered Finlay a new range of scales, levels and viewpoints as well as tones and textures. His famous inscriptions on wood or stone – quotations evoking the whole range of Western civilization – are buried in the ground, built into walls and perched in trees, the crowns of which can

BELOW For the terraced gardens at the Rou Estate in Corfu, designers Jennifer Gay and Piers Goldson chose plants such as santolina and *Tulbaghia violacea* that would be tolerant of drought, thin soil and the heat reflected from drystone walls in midsummer.

also be seen from above. The lines of terracing are themselves like waves, one of the artist's favourite images. But Fleur de l'Air is in no sense a sculpture park.[11] The careful placing of Finlay's artefacts makes the most of each landscape variation all down the hillside, open or sheltered, structured or loosely patterned. They blend into the setting and become part of its fabric. Some are small-scaled and half-hidden, present in the garden like birdsong or the sound of water. Others are large and imposing, like the assemblage of granite slabs, similar to those dramatically deployed on Finlay's Scottish moor, here strung out in a curved line below a terrace wall. The surrounding wild grass is mowed to accentuate the linearity. In both Scotland and Provence, Finlay carefully avoided giving his inscriptions the centrality that visiting photographers so often prefer. He frequently insisted that, 'whereas a conventional artwork exists as an independent object, the environmental or garden artwork is incomplete, perhaps even incomprehensible, apart from its surroundings'[12] – just as in concrete poetry, space complements words. Terracing at Fleur de l'Air imposes linear, narrative discovery, but no single itinerary dominates. The owners themselves take a different route each time they visit. Their hillside cannot be seen from outside the property so that exploration must be from within.

Finlay was one of the first moderns to reject land artist Robert Smithson's claim that 'art degenerates as it approaches gardening'. The Scottish artist insisted on the contrary that 'the art of gardening is like the art

Fleur de l'Air, Provence | Ian Hamilton Finlay
'Declaration' (opposite), a quotation from the French historian Jules Michelet, inscribed on granite slabs along a narrow terrace. On a bronze plaque among the olive prunings (below), 'Mercury, god of the roads, give our ankles wings'. Ian Hamilton Finlay loved 'translating verticals into horizontals'.

of writing, of painting, of sculpture; it is the art of composing, and making a harmony, with disparate elements'. His vocabulary can be resolutely Romantic: 'Superior gardens are composed of glooms and solitudes and not of plants and trees.'[13] But Finlay cannot be easily labelled. His half-obscure, half-obscured quotations, set among the rocks and trees, are full of humour, irony and ambiguity of reference. In no sense was his art, as Hunt points out, romantically 'egocentric' or limited to 'self-extension'. Hunt concludes that 'Finlay's designs always bring the immediate, the near and the local into dialogue with the distant, the far and the universal'.

For Hunt, Finlay's work answers positively the essential question: 'Can gardening and place making serve ends beyond their own aesthetic ambitions and physical materiality?'[14] The efforts of Nicole de Vésian on similarly terraced hillsides may seem modest compared to Finlay's – literal and domestic rather than metaphorical. Vésian, part Provençal, part

Welsh, began to garden in Provence at the age of seventy after a legendary career in interior design. She deliberately avoided anything conceptual: 'I like to create on roots. I like things to be logical but also part of everyday life. I hate pretension, gratuity. I am close to the earth, I have my feet on the ground, I want everything I create to be practical, logical, rational – an ideal not far removed from that of good design. There is no reason things can't be both practical and beautiful.'[15] The blending of use and beauty is essential to all vernacular art as well as being characteristically Mediterranean. Victor Papanek, the vernacular's great defender, insisted that design had become the most powerful instrument 'with which man shapes his tools and environments (and, by extension, society and himself)'. Vésian's gardens are moreover just as Virgilian or Homeric as Finlay's. Neither of these ancient poets separated poetry from domestic concerns. Princess Nausicaa, after all, was washing laundry when she met Odysseus.[16]

Clos Pascal, Provence | Nicole de Vésian

On this steeply terraced hillside, the site itself is the work, its walls rebuilt, contours reshaped, trees thinned. Outside edges and connections between levels require special attention. Each space keeps its character, but all combine fragments of old fields, spontaneous growth, weathered objects of stone and wood, with formally clipped evergreens.

Vésian and Finlay had much in common: she, too, made one great iconic garden, her own (La Louve), but also worked elsewhere. Neither was above manual labour but, on the contrary, loved to dig and build. Both began with what was already there, making the most of the place's existing character. Both, as Finlay put it, embarked 'on a garden with a Vision but never a plan'.[17] The Visions of both were powerful and personal, hard to imitate, but both artists were present in their creations only indirectly, never in a self-parading manner. For both, houses count as a central focus, unrepentant evidence of the human presence, but one which neither dominates nor determines the overall layout. On terraced hillsides, both designers made good use of plunging views but also of long horizontal perspectives alternating with mysterious interruptions. Both let paths meander, deliberately multidirectional, not haphazardly, but without hierarchy. Both had a sense of almost mischievous play, enticing and misleading. Both disdained sentimental pastoral and rustic pastiche.

The differences between them are nonetheless striking, revealed nowhere better than in each artist's treatment of rock and stone. Finlay had his slabs of granite imported at great expense from Scotland, already inscribed with a quotation from the French writer Jules Michelet: 'We would wish to engrave our law on the stone of eternal right, on the rock that brings the world invariable justice and indestructible equity.' Vésian's art is local and non-verbal. She mixed natural outcrops, drystone remnants, stones salvaged in fields by local farmers when ploughing and fragments of rustic sculpture. Her 'quotations' are vestiges of earlier life on the site or allusions to larger landscape patterns, typical of the region since Roman times. The American designer Garrett Finney, who in recent years has added a pool to Vésian's garden at La Louve and whose own work ranges from space capsules and camping cars to wrought iron, admired in Vésian the 'integration of the exceptional within the vernacular'.[18] Vésian and Finlay shared one very important thing, however: for both, their own gardens were 'less a place than a world'.[19]

La Louve, Provence | Nicole de Vésian
On the small, dry terraces of her own garden, Vésian mixed stone and plants as equal partners. La Louve is a garden for year-round living, not a showcase.

La Louve, Provence | Nicole de Vésian

Garrett Finney's swimming pool (left), a later addition, was carefully adapted to vernacular inspiration. Vésian (below) imagined a kind of cobbled village street running through her house and out to the road beyond, linking her to the larger landscape and site history.

3
EARTHWORKS

Creating means giving form to the formless. Destroying is reducing form to dust. What better matter for creating than earth which is everywhere available? It is the most commonplace matter and at the same time the richest in dust, the richest in the memory of forms.

Giuseppe Penone, contemporary Italian sculptor[1]

Vernacular architecture has always made much of very local building materials. The southern French peasant writer Adrienne Cazeilles remembers how, in her childhood, 'Each person built the size house he required, according to the dictates of climate, slope and the nature of the soil. Each used the cheapest possible materials, those found on the spot, showing the colour of the soil of the particular place that provided them. All of this gave each community its specific character, its perfect adaptation to a local model.'[2] This human practice is part of a larger diversity, that 'veritable cornucopia of habitats'[3] that characterizes any Mediterranean ecosystem, each of which (including human) evolves to fit local conditions of weather, soil and topography. The Mediterranean fabric is so complex that produce grown mere metres apart may vary greatly in taste and smell,[4] a fact exploited by vintners to produce wines linked to very local *terroirs*. At the same time, it is earth that directly provides the raw materials for much vernacular art: for roof and floor tiles, glazes, washes, various dyes for fabrics, pots and dishes of all kinds, and many of the pigments used by painters. Many places are famous especially for the extraction and multiple uses of 'terra rossa', ferruginous sediments that accumulated in pockets when the sea withdrew, especially on its northern rim.

PAGE 54 Earthenware jars at Al Hossoun in Morocco are never mere planters but are left empty to be admired in their own right.

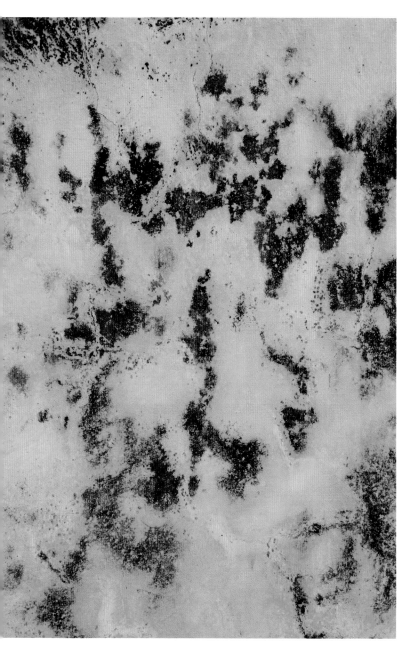

OPPOSITE, LEFT AND ABOVE Pockets of iron oxide around the Mediterranean tinge earth red and provide warm tones for washes and rendered walls, as here in Mallorca.

PIGMENTS

Northern painters such as Delacroix and Van Gogh came south in search of strong colour and light. The potent southern sun[5] that makes wine strong and fragrance intense still draws visitors who are looking for sensuous primitivism or 'earthiness'. In Provence, the Souleiado fabric company adjusted its colour range from the duller, darker traditional tones to warmer ones when it began to sell worldwide, and to tourists. Newcomers to Provence sometimes paint their holiday homes bright orange with lavender-blue shutters. Jean Giono objected strenuously to this phenomenon already in the 1950s, rejecting the 'gaudy patchwork' of the Rhône valley, 'the candy pink of peach trees, the vulgar yellow of rape fields and the red of poppies', adding: 'Don't believe the painter who stuffs this country with blood red, gold yellow and vinegar green. Everything is grey.'[6] In fact, this is a false problem: the effects of colour in the landscape, bright or muted, depend on use and context, and especially on illumination. The Anglo-Greek novelist and gardener Petrie Harbouri notes: 'What makes the brilliance of scarlet hibiscus, orange campsis, magenta bougainvillea so satisfying is their luminosity. The same colours printed on cloth or paper would be flat and merely garish, but the petals of flowers are lambent, impregnated with light.'[7]

ABOVE A beautiful Bird of Paradise (*Caesalpinia gilliesii*) in the Dar Igdad garden in Morocco is enhanced by changing light from hour to hour.

Painter Paul Cézanne, an indigenous but hardly regionalist painter, pushed the exploration of strong earth colours, of grey and of luminosity to new limits. In 1895, he rented a cabin in the abandoned quarry site of Bibémus in the Mont Sainte-Victoire, near his native city, Aix-en-Provence, the better to paint its rough geometries. In 1987, the French classical scholar Jacqueline de Romilly, who had a house nearby, described this quarry as 'huge slices of rock, sometimes pale grey and sometimes violent red, profiled against the green of the pines in bold contrasts of volume and colour that are almost abstract and yet very real'.[8] In 1998, Bibémus became city property and has been sensitively restored by landscape architect Philippe Deliau and his team at the ALEP agency. Their work respects the geological configuration, the social history

THIS PAGE Among the brilliant flowers displayed in the garden at Al Hossoun in Morocco are *Solandra grandiflora*, or chalice vine (below); a bougainvillea cultivar from Burma (right); *Brugmansia aurea* (bottom left); and *Brugmansia x candida* (bottom right).

of the quarry's exploitation from the seventeenth to the nineteenth centuries, and its role in the Cézanne legend. They aimed first at changing the site as little as possible, making paths with structures that could be easily removed or repositioned – larchwood boardwalks, oak steps and ramps in wrought iron or Corten. These remain very discreet but allow visitors to discover the 1.3-kilometre circuit without contributing to further erosion. The ALEP team also edited cross views and perspectives (some onto other parts of the Mont Sainte-Victoire), beautifully framing and organizing successive planes and volumes, using mainly diagonals. The varied green foliage of pines, arbutus and oaks softens the geometric contours. The result is a giant landscape sculpture that embraces Cézanne's vision but has very much its own identity and strength, a new work of landscape art in its own right.

Bibémus, Provence | Philippe Deliau, ALEP Agency
This famous geological and historic site inspired the painter Paul Cézanne. Today, discreet and ingenious intervention has transformed it into a stunning sculpted landscape accessible to a wide public.

RAMMED EARTH

In southern Morocco, rammed earth has been a traditional building material for thousands of years. In the seventeenth century, it was used to build the 7.5-kilometre-long ramparts of Taroudant, with their hundred and thirty towers and five vaulted gates. The city is of course much older: it was a centre of Tuareg resistance to Roman invaders, a rich caravan trading centre for salt, sugar and cotton, a Jewish holy city, and, much later, a French protectorate (1912–56). It sits along the dry mud flats of Oued Souss River, between two ranges of mountains, the Grand Atlas to the north and the Anti-Atlas to the south, bordering the Sahara. Taroudant gets both Atlantic mists and the ochre light of the desert. A few decades ago, its ramparts and houses were washed a bright red, while many local women still wore robes of

BELOW The rammed earth ramparts of Taroudant, usually brown and beige, turn red and brilliant in the setting sun. Behind, in silhouette, are the Atlas mountains.

Tuareg indigo. Then a governor decreed that all town buildings would keep the natural tone of the region's soil, a rich brown, leaving brighter hues to the more touristy town of Marrakech to the north.

No such law restricts the use of coloured washes in private domains outside town. Since 2003, a whole series of such properties has been elaborated by landscape designers Arnaud Maurières and Eric Ossart, who use rammed earth as their main construction material. In these complexes, houses, courtyards and gardens are inextricably linked. This nomadic pair has for decades been exploring the Paradise gardens of Andalusia, the Romanesque churches of Lebanon, the patios and castles of Syria, the cloisters and Arabo-Norman palaces of Sicily, collecting enough pottery, baskets, tent hangings and carpets along the way to fill several books and two museums.[9] They feel that southern Morocco is truly Mediterranean: 'It is essentially fed by eastern Mediterranean influences and authorities today situate the origin of the Berber peoples on the northern shores of this same Mediterranean.' They recall that Fernand Braudel considered the desert an essential frontier of the region. But they add, 'This is a Mediterranean without the sea, a world of earth and wind, of farming and irrigation, of fresh running water, of fruit swollen with sugar and sun, and fragrant flowers.'[10]

Al Hossoun, Morocco | Arnaud Maurières and Eric Ossart
The design duo admire both the Mexican Luis Barragán and the Brazilian Roberto Burle Marx. The latter, says Maurières, 'showed us how to reconcile botany and art in the garden'.

Maurières and Ossart's most ambitious project in Morocco is Al Hossoun, a sequence of six, cloister-like courtyards covering some 6,300 square metres, each with its own type of planting. Recently the property was purchased by a consortium of garden lovers from Avignon to make a guest lodge. The new owners appreciate the designers' knowledge of vernacular skills to the point of planning a small museum on site to display leftover bricks and tiles, with explanations of production techniques.

Rammed earth construction provides excellent insulation for both heat and cold. Teams building such walls go very fast, stacking and pounding the earth between wooden frames. Upkeep consists mainly in keeping out water infiltration from above or below. In Taroudant, a centuries-old rampart tower recently tumbled down because, in this region where the

annual rainfall is ten centimetres, seventeen fell in a few hours... In rammed earth architecture, one cube is one room. But in these courtyard sequences, space keeps being subdivided, so that there is rarely a general viewpoint, simply a gradual unveiling. Even doors, set deeply and invitingly under arches, often contain smaller doors in the larger frame. The outdoor spaces, even when broad and open, are completely circumscribed. Only the sky is visible from within the enclosures, except from roof terraces.

Water is an essential part of the design, but pools are kept low and discreet, empty of plants that would disturb reflections of the sky. Light reflected from water dances on inside ceilings. All the surfaces of the hammams and bathrooms are coated with *tadelakht*, a semi-shiny, water-resistant finish made entirely of lime. The earth it requires is brought from Marrakech, the only source that, as Eric Ossart notes, gives something 'soft and fresh all at once, very human'. It is easy to refinish invisibly if necessary. The designers like to extend bathrooms outdoors in tiny individual courtyard gardens, watered by the run-off from showers and sinks. Sometimes there is even a shower head hidden among the greenery.

Stonecutting is not a local speciality, but once, when seeking out ancient stone threshing floors in the Anti-Atlas mountains, Maurières and Ossart came upon a team of men actually building one. Their method is the same as the one used to construct roads in Roman times: huge blocks are buried at least forty centimetres deep, then the cracks are filled in with chips and earth. The designers managed to hire these same workmen to make paths for their courtyards. The team comes now as needed, bringing its own stone, charging by the square metre of finished work.

Maurières and Ossart love earth colours. They have also long admired Mexican architect Luis Barragán and, while many of their constructions keep their natural colour, Barragán's inspiration appears in accents such as a red wall rising above a sea of greenery or between the trunks of palms, or a pale façade setting off a shady door. Near Taroudant, the pair explored the foothills for different qualities and tones of earth, and then experimented with red, white and green pigments. The earth samples were mixed with lime and chopped straw to make a thick rendering. Because the green was disappointing, and certain reds turned soft pink and were difficult to touch up invisibly (something often required), the designers

Al Hossoun, Morocco | Arnaud Maurières and Eric Ossart
At the heart of the garden is the long pool, unplanted but
surrounded by exotic luxuriance. All the hardscape makes
use of vernacular skills.

decided finally to keep 'white' earth – in fact, a very soft beige – for certain façades and indoor walls, using pure lime for the most brilliant. This method gives gentler tones than an alternative approach: the simple blending of lime and water to create a wash for walls already coated, coloured with natural oxides found at Imintanoute in the High Atlas mountains.

For earthenware tiles, Maurières and Ossart discovered a dying village that had for centuries provided oil and water jars for city trade. Here they work with one family in particular. Typically, they choose a grey-green glaze usually reserved for cookware to make floor tiles for their hammams, reinventing as well as preserving. Bricks from this village are also used indoors and out, for example as edging for gravel paths. Earthenware in their courtyards also takes the form of *claustras*, triangular separation walls modelled after those of Andalusian tobacco factories, another sub-division of space to mask and invite. Pots, glazed and unglazed,

Al Hossoun, Morocco | Arnaud Maurières and Eric Ossart

Persian influence shows here in the subtle and continuous subdivision of spaces, mysteriously glimpsed through and beyond, with beautiful patterning and soft colour variations as in a carpet.

are common all over, never planted but grouped as art objects in their own right. Such vernacular productions are always irregular, each object unique. The designers like to mix them with the geometries of tinted concrete, thus avoiding the Mediterranean clichés of 'pebble paving, pergolas and terracotta pots'.

In their plantings, Maurières and Ossart also make use of local resources in unusual ways. They discovered in Morocco a thornless variety of opuntia, the roadside cactus, which makes good jam. Eric raids old fields of agaves planted under the French protectorate for the production of fibre, and now long abandoned. But the pair also hunt plants worldwide, scouting in Burma, Madagascar and Mexico to find varieties suitable for Taroudant. They love to combine species with similar needs but originating on different continents. Although they do not like cactus gardens as such, they now mix American species with South African euphorbias, grasses like their much-loved *Hyparrhenia hirta* and others, unnamed, that grow wild in the Sahara. Flowers are always present, often as climbers, such as the orange-flowered *Pyrostegia venusta* underplanted with yellow-flowered, wild *Aloe vera* from Tunisia.

Arnaud Maurières and Eric Ossart practise a kind of fusion art, plucking their *claustras* and pools from Andalusia, their plants from Burma or Madagascar. But just as each plant's needs are respected in its new environment, so the original function of traditional materials and techniques contribute to their current use: the garden paths laid in stone are as solid as Roman roads. 'What we do,' says Arnaud, 'is a contemporary adaptation of a vocabulary initiated in the Middle East long before Moslems disseminated it throughout the Mediterranean basin. We wanted to make gardens like those, where everything is reference and symbol, but adapted to today's needs. This we have done, in a way that lets us go beyond, to free ourselves from these references and symbols and open up to other models, other plants, to tell our own story in a new kind of oasis.'[11]

Al Hossoun, Morocco | Arnaud Maurières and Eric Ossart
The quarry from which earth was extracted to make the buildings has been left open to the sky, like a giant, dry swimming pool. This sunken garden provides a spectacular display space, where fast-growing bananas and papayas provide shade for tender exotics.

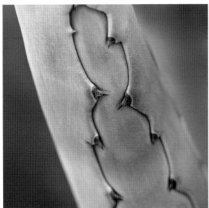

ABOVE At Dar Igdad, the property next door to Al Hossoun, Arnaud Maurières and Eric Ossart experimented with a vast, drought-tolerant 'meadow', mixing American agaves, African euphorbias and Saharan grasses.

WOODWORKS

Seek not a statue wrought by Dadedalis or Plyclitus, or by Phradmon
carved or Ageladas, but the rough-hewn trunk of some old tree which
you may venerate as god Priapus in your garden's midst...[1]

Columella, *De Re Rustica*, first century AD

Trees may be grouped in gardens or landscapes as groves, glades, copses, park, woodland, forest or wilderness. Plantings may be miniature or vast, regular or haphazard, monospecies or mixed. All have ever been endowed by humans with a wide range of social and religious connotations.[2] The south differs from the north in important ways. Firstly, the biodiversity experts explain that: 'Beginning as early as the Neolithic, the history of the Mediterranean forest is one of terrible cycles of destruction and regeneration. Enormous amounts of wood were used in the course of history for such varied purposes as domestic firewood, furniture, charcoal, shipbuilding, other forms of construction, and clearing of land for agriculture and livestock husbandry. By the seventh century AD, the entire Mediterranean Basin was transformed to timber-based industries.'[3] Nonetheless, both the scientists and the historians Horden and Purcell agree that degradation has regularly alternated with 'secondary recovery', linked to 'the small-scaled heterogeneity of Mediterranean living, so dependent on local and ever changing conditions'.[4] Forests grow back and indeed are currently closing up many northern Mediterranean landscapes. They are still, however, marked by exceptional diversity: 'There are approximately 290 species of trees in the region, of which more than 200 are endemics … by contrast, there are only 135 species in all of central and northern Europe.'[5]

There is another important difference between north and south: in the Mediterranean region, 'the term "forest" should not 'bring to mind an image of high, dense stands of trees with a closed canopy. Few such forests exist in the region today and probably have never been common in the past.' Even at their prehistoric peak, 'Mediterranean landscapes have tended to be rather open and heterogeneous', favouring 'a more open formation, sometimes called "woodland" or "park woodland"'.[6] Horden and Purcell use the term 'integrated Mediterranean forest' to describe a locally managed, sustainable model that provides fuel, food for domestic animals, wildlife for food, plants with a thousand uses, wood for curing meat, minerals and even plague remedies.[7] A southern French landscape historian, Christian Tamisier, concurs: 'Our wooded hills are luminous, dry and prickly, but circumscribed, familiar, oft-explored.'[8] This is a far cry from the northern picturesque vision of British architect William Gilpin (c. 1780): 'The forest disdains all human culture.'[9]

PAGE 70 In a beautifully thinned holm oak grove in Provence, a giant sphere by Marc Nucera gives new life to a willow that died nearby.

OPPOSITE Around the medieval Prieuré Saint-Symphorien in Provence, Nicole de Vésian simply thinned and pruned existing oaks and undergrowth, mainly wild box, setting off mossy rocks. The gardened grove becomes a distillation of the breathtaking woodland beyond.

GLADE AND GROVE

If Mediterranean woodland was domestic, groves were often sacred, especially around springs. Horden and Purcell describe the ancient 'religion of the productive landscape',[10] in which sacred groves were not 'just a sprinkling of cult places like a kind of seasoning' but part of an all-inclusive veneration, which did not separate human activity from wild nature. When Odysseus was finally grounded at Phaecea, Athena led him to rest 'beneath two shoots of olive that grew from a single stock – the one an ungrafted sucker, while the other had been grafted'.[11] The historians point out that, although 'it is often thought that what Mediterranean

culture has articulated is a sharp division between the desert and the sown, between productive terrain and wilderness ... on closer inspection, instead of a dichotomy, we find here two ends of a finely calibrated scale'.[12] Sanctuary trees might be wild, cultivated or both. No single species represents the continuum better than the olive, whose exact origins are still unknown. This species rarely lent itself to Romantic fancy: the French novelist Stendhal claimed in 1838 that 'no tree in the world could be uglier; it always looks doddery and stunted'.[13] Roughly a hundred years later, the British writer Aldous Huxley deemed that the olive tree belongs to 'a region of sun-lit clarity separating the damps of the equator from the damps of the North. It is the symbol of a classicism enclosed between two romanticisms.'[14]

BELOW Near Rome today, olive groves, woodbelts and pastures, seen from a ridge of dry scrubland. Olive trees were once widely spaced to allow for intercropping with vines and cereal crops.

ABOVE At Trabari in Provence, a graded view from clipped trees (*Quercus ilex*) to unpruned crowns to distant cliffs, occupied by humans since pre-history. The designer Nicole de Vésian loved to play with degrees of human intervention in Mediterranean landscapes, evolving through time.

OPPOSITE A grove on Corfu. In 'Seven Definitions Pertaining to Ideal Landscape', Ian Hamilton Finlay defined 'grove' as 'an irregular peristyle'.

Fleur de l'Air, Provence | Ian Hamilton Finlay

Finlay's temple rises between grove and glade. Nothing here
implies 'wilderness'; rather, the scene's many allusions suggest
human communion with nature since antiquity.

Groves, in European parks and gardens from
the sixteenth to the mid-eighteenth century, alternated with representations of 'wilderness' as different
moods within a single property. Italian usage con-
trasted the 'barco' or park and the smaller 'boschetto', grove or 'minia-
turized, symbolic wood'. The latter often contained allegorical sculptures,
a temple or a fountain, with explicit allusions to classical precedents.
The 'boschetto' continued to offer refreshing shade and cool water and
ensured relative privacy, but not yet 'solitude', which would later become
the Romantic hallmark.[15] In the eighteenth-century English landscape
garden, the 'temple in a glade' gradually became a standard feature, more
and more 'subsumed into the landscape garden scene to form a satisfying
narrative whole, rather than boldly presented as stand-alone set pieces
in the landscape'.[16]

Ian Hamilton Finlay created such a temple at Fleur de l'Air in Provence (see also pp. 45–48). The grove had been a constant fascination for the poet from his beginnings, even 'a kind of Platonic form...'. Finlay had already embellished an olive orchard at the Parco di Celle near Pistoia to create 'The Virgilian Wood'.[17] His work inspired an American artist in Tuscany, Sheppard Craige, to create Il Bosco della Ragnaia, another interpretation of the grove.

The temple at Fleur de l'Air is exquisitely situated between olive terraces and light woodland, grove and glade combined, both inextricably 'natural' and 'cultural'. Around the temple, the inscription *L'Ombra media sulla luce* ('Shadows muse on light') suggests metaphysical dimensions but connects them to hourly and seasonal change, and especially weather. Finlay loved weather. Among his disconnected sentences can be found: 'In the whole of philosophy, there is almost no weather'; 'Weather is the chief content of a garden'; and also 'Weather is a third to place and time'.[18]

Jacqueline Morabito, born on the French Riviera, has also transformed a hillside where glade shades into grove, light woodland into olive terracing. Like Nicole de Vésian, Morabito is a designer of everyday objects – dishes, furniture, jewelry, as well as display spaces for museums and shops. At the top of her hill stands a mix of Aleppo pines and white and green oaks. Just a few trees are shaped here, anticipating the elegant graphic patterning further down. In the spaces circumscribed by ancient limestone walls, Morabito has clipped and shaped broadleaf evergreen shrubs, alternating foliage with bared wood and pale stone to create visual rhythms all over the site (see also pp. 98–102). A stone circle is laid in

The Grove, French Riviera | Jacqueline Morabito
Morabito has thinned the upper pine wood and shaped its undergrowth into flowing forms (above). A witty woodpile (left) dialogues with the lines, tones and textures of the stone wall behind.

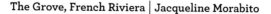

rough grass next to a rounded clump of wild lentisk (*Pistacia lentiscus*). A low stacked woodpile makes a ring around a tree. Rectangles and circles, cubes and spheres are organized from ground to roof level. Such subtle art needs little water, but Morabito uses drip irrigation to create contrasts in summer between circles of green (watered) grass and the naturally sere tones of everything else in the summer heat. Though she mainly edits, she has added common boxwood and a line of cypresses. Finlay's additions may be half hidden, and dependent on siting for their effects, but they are clearly artefacts. Morabito's contributions, as is so often the case in Mediterranean landscape art today, blend seamlessly with what was already present. It is really impossible, in many places, to determine where she began. The whole site becomes sculpture, but is still agricultural. Her centuries-old olive trees are pruned to encourage production, but, typically, she adds to their bounty the fruit of small wild olives that survive among the pines and oaks. 'They have almost no flesh,' she explains, 'but they contribute incomparable flavour.'

Morabito says her role is 'to make sublime what is already there'. Her work is called 'minimalist' because of her emphasis on strong, simple volumes alternating with uncluttered space and clean lines. John Dixon Hunt considers that Finlay 'deliberately occupied an ambiguous zone between modernism and neoclassicism'[19] that can be linked to minimalism. Finlay certainly rejected the 'fussy particulars' of today's gardening fashions in favour of the 'grave generalizations' of 'classical gardens'. Morabito is not alluding to a classical past so much as perpetuating it. Like Finlay's Eurydice, she celebrates directly her woods, stars, nightingales, clouds, oaks, rocks and groves. For both, however, the sublime approaches the sacred. Finlay once wrote that 'the highest aim is not art but a kind of piety'. Jean Giono recalls that on Sundays, in old Provençal villages, when the women went to mass on Sundays, the men went, as to worship, to the olive groves.[20]

The Grove, French Riviera | Jacqueline Morabito
On the olive terraces and in the small vineyard, changing light brings out subtle variations in texture and tone. This work, if not exactly sacred, still pays homage to the 'religion of the productive landscape'.

TREES

Aldous Huxley loves the olive tree for its admirable 'clarity and definition ... associated with a certain physical spareness. Most of the great deciduous trees of England give one the impression, at any rate in summer, of being rather obese... By comparison the olive tree seems an athlete in training.'[21] This clarity is again the result of pruning, a vernacular art recognized as such since ancient times. The Roman agronomist Columella praises the 'pruner perched amid the trees' along with the 'gardener working in his verdant plot',[22] as two peas in the same pod. Romantic sensibilities consider all pruning a mutilation, or at least an exercise in domination (see pp. 87 ff.). It is certainly true that there are various approaches to pruning, and some are both excessive and destructive. But fruit trees and vines need human help not only to thrive and produce but even to survive. Left without human care, they waste energy making wood, sicken from lack of light, dwindle and die.

One artist in Provence embodies in his own life and work this link between agriculture and art. Marc Nucera was admired early in his career by Christine Picasso as a 'sculptor of living plants'. His father was a furniture maker who once won a prestigious national competition for woodworking. Nucera himself originally trained in arboriculture in two technical schools near Avignon. His first big job was the restoration of a vast orchard of five-hundred-year-old olive trees near Toulon. Here

ABOVE At this private *mas* in Provence, dark pine woodland backs silvery olive foliage, juxtaposed by Marc Nucera in three different ways: as a working grove, as flat-topped individuals, and pruned into a staggered line of dancing shapes.

he learned that 'trees, to produce, must be happy, and happy trees are beautiful'. His aim ever since has been to sense, respect and enhance the dynamics of each individual specimen. In 1992, he went into business for himself as a 'landscape pruner' and in 1995 won an award for best crafts-man of his *département*. He then began to work with two great masters of Mediterranean landscape art: Nicole de Vésian and her pupil at that time, Alain David Idoux. Vésian gave Nucera his first camera, suggesting that he take pictures from the tops of trees he was shaping. She also encour-aged him to make child-like stick drawings to bring out essential connec-tions. Above all, she showed him the art of perceiving a sculpted specimen against a landscape so that its forms and curves would echo and answer those be-yond. His favourite species for work *in situ* are the holm oak, almond, olive, stone pine, juniper and plane

BELOW In this Bastide garden in Provence, an olive grove planted by Alain David Idoux in around 1995 follows the valley's irregular contours. Marc Nucera transformed a dead cedar into silver pebbles to connect the grove, playfully but effectively, to the formal garden.

trees. He avoids making individual trees central: the spaces between and around count as much as the tree's silhouette, the tracery of its branches and the masses of its foliage.

Nucera is sensitive in all his work to a dynamic that unites growth and decay. From the beginning, he pruned trees with a view to future development. This meant return visits, sometimes over years. In recent times, he has worked more and more with trees that are already dead. Those that are still part of a larger landscape become part of the site and continue to evolve. Sculpting a hundred-year-old pine overcome by insect invasion, he wrote a poem imagining the thoughts of the decaying tree: 'My body now feeds myriad forms of new life[...] I die and live again in so many different ways.'[23] One of these ways is art – even if only for a time.

One of Nucera's most impressive works with dead trees is on the cliff of the Carmejane gardens in Provence. This part of the property had once been a village garbage dump. Roughly covered with dirt and wildflowers, it released debris with every heavy rain. Dauntless American owners removed four hundred tons of refuse to uncover wonderful rock shapes, now colonized by mosses and lichens. Here Nucera 'Walkers', upside-down trees chosen for their character, seem to stride across the promontory. Nucera also makes furniture with plane tree wood, using the giant trunks of healthy trees cut down to widen roads. But here, too, he preserves the memory of the tree, since each set could, theoretically, be reassembled like a puzzle into the shape of the original trunk. Some of his finest examples are at the Domaine de la Verrière in the Mont Ventoux region, a recently restored winery that has brought new life to an abandoned hamlet. In one place, a line of sculpted pines moves from dead trees to living. In another, a circle of sculpted trunks set under living canopies has been baptized 'Wood Henge'. In the sculptures he is now making in his own garden, densely worked masses fretted with a chain saw, Nucera feels he is working with the very energy

Mas de Michel, Provence | Marc Nucera

On this open farmland (below), Nucera organized his weather-worn pebbles into a serpentine to lead the eye towards the silver rocks of the Alpilles. His work is inseparable from its surroundings, and is often designed on site.

Le Terrain, Provence | Marc Nucera

Views of the artist's outdoor studio (opposite). Nucera learned from Nicole de Vésian how to balance shapes, textures and soft tones of wood, foliage and stone. Dynamic, weathered volumes change with light and weather in semi-wild settings.

La Carmejane, Provence | Marc Nucera

An upended pine tree (below) dances along the cliff front between the hilltown above and the garden below. Rough nature again blends seamlessly into human manufacture. Dead trees thus achieve new life, though not forever.

BELOW RIGHT Sculpture at a *mas* in Provence. When Marc Nucera sculpts wooden blocks, he seeks to free each one's inherent, dynamic character. His work gives equal importance to volume and void. Setting is crucial, angles of vision multiple.

of matter, directed by the fibres of the tree as he is, in the landscape, by the larger dynamics of density and space.[24]

Nucera, like the British tree sculptor David Nash, identifies 'with the time and energy of the tree and with its mortality'.[25] This, however, can mean different things to different people. The Italian artist Giuseppe Penone expresses his own sense of identification by marking natural objects, most often trees, with the imprint of his own body.[25] In his series 'Alpes Maritimes' (1968), a tree is forced to grow around a bronze cast of the artist's hand inserted through its trunk, its growth stopped – as the artist notes with satisfaction – at that point. Another bears the contour of the artist's body outlined in nails. The latter work is labelled 'The Tree Will Remember the Contact'.[26] The identity explored in these works is entirely the artist's own. No report mentions the species, age or aspect of the tree, still less its setting. Nucera and Morabito know intimately the needs of each particular species, and their pruning encourages each individual's natural growth habit. To the imperious 'penetration' of one identity at the expense of the other, they prefer an art that is genuinely interactive, a dialogue of benefit to both.

Le Terrain | Marc Nucera

Another plane tree trunk has its energies unleashed. The blue colour comes from the copper spray used as a fungicide by organic fruit growers and vintners since the nineteenth century.

ABOVE A stand of oaks by Marc Nucera at the famous mountain winery of Domaine de la Verrière in Provence. The first tree, dead, still exhorts passers-by. The second is half sculpted, the next less so, until free-form, living trees complete the line.

CLIPPED GREENERY

5

It is hard to explain to the modern garden-lover, whose conception of the charm of gardens is formed of successive pictures of flower-loveliness, how this effect of enchantment can be produced by anything so dull and monotonous as a mere combination of clipped greenery and stonework.

Edith Wharton, *Italian Villas and their Gardens*, 1904[1]

Southern light is the first sculptor of space. At its strongest, it creates stark confrontations between lit and shaded areas, volumes and planes, obscuring detail and colour. During a long stay in Jerusalem, the English designer Dan Pearson 'learned to love the dramatic reduction back to the absolute essentials. The light, the intensity of contrast in the shadow and the process of learning to retrain your eye was a revelation.'[2] The Anglo-Greek gardener Caroline Harbouri, pondering Greek landscapes, similarly observed: 'Attica taught me to understand that the beauty of gardens in this climate depends more upon shape and form, the play of light and shade, and indeed on scent, rather than on lushness and profuse colour.'[3] Such effects of almost monochrome contrast have been exploited for centuries in parks and gardens that limit their vocabulary, in the main, to stonework and clipped greenery.

Not just any greenery: according to the biodiversity researchers, Mediterranean-type ecosystems worldwide are characterized by a preponderance of broadleaf evergreen trees and shrubs belonging to unrelated plant families but sharing similar characteristics, especially foliage that limits evaporation by being tough, waxy or spiny.[4] Many of them concentrate their moisture into essential oils rich in fragrance. Such species include the olive, cypress, holm oak (*Quercus ilex*), bay tree (*Laurus nobilis*), strawberry tree (*Arbutus unedo*), lentisk (*Pistacia lentiscus*), common boxwood (*Buxus sempervirens*) and laurustinus (*Viburnum tinus*). The leaves of these shrubs and small trees may remain on the plant for two or three years, another effective strategy for saving water. These species also share 'remarkable regenerative abilities after severe stress (fire, cutting, disease, etc.)', and most take beautifully to shaping and pruning. In some, dull leathery foliage absorbs light, while in others, shinier textures reflect it. Artists, designers and gardeners play on the differences of texture and luminosity in foliage as with stone. In the parks of earlier centuries, formal design was largely architectural, concerned with axes, perspectives and symmetry. Participating plants lost their individual

PAGE 86 Traditional cypress windbreaks often disappear when farms become holiday homes. Marc Nucera transformed this one at a private *mas* in Provence into landscape art – not topiary, because he follows natural growth rather than imposing a preconceived form.

ABOVE Surrounding a plane tree pruned in the traditional manner to provide summer shade, Nicole de Vésian assembled a tapestry of grey and green spheres, fragrant and tactile, restful in summer, and a presence year round.

identity. The contemporary version of the *ferme ornée* (see p. 126) often favours adaptations of this style to contemporary tastes, more playful and open-ended.

In northern parks and gardens, box parterres and broderies are considered the direct opposite of free-form, naturalistic floral plantings. Today, moreover, it is common to dismiss clipped greenery as sterile, rigid and boringly predictable. But the relationship between 'formal' and 'natural' is different in the south, where box is first of all a wild, scrubland plant that self-sows over acres of dry

ABOVE At Le Clos Pascal in Provence, a traditional courtyard fountain with clipped box, cypress and pine. Plantings carefully avoid symmetry but maintain harmony. Nicole de Vésian rarely features water, barely visible here. Stone and plants are her medium.

hills. On such sites, broadleaf evergreens are already mounded by wind, drought, sheep, fire and frost. Humans make use of these tough species for windbreaks, and it is practical necessity that first imposes lines and patterns. When architects and sculptors then organize them into shapes and masses, topiary and parterres, they are not choosing artifice over nature, the tame versus the wild, but merely going one step further than the farmers into human intervention. The very same plants participate at every stage of the continuum, from spontaneous 'nature' to the most contrived 'art'. The same progression works with stone: existing outcrops and found rocks are incorporated into drystone sustaining walls and buildings for practical reasons, then sculpted into balustrades and statuary for parks and gardens. Water also exists spontaneously as the run-off of torrential rains or the capricious output of springs. Farmers collect it in reservoirs or cisterns; architects make fountains and pools. The continuum with stone and water is commonplace elsewhere, but the plant connection is specifically Mediterranean because of the region's characteristic vegetation. Clipping comes, so to speak, naturally. Even roadmenders in remote areas of the south prune wild box, laurel, oaks and viburnum for the sheer fun of it. No one assumes that clipping means control. These evergreens grow lustily and steadily, especially in mild winter weather, so that shaping must begin over and over again.

Artists drawn to the vernacular idiom often explore this deep link between 'wild' and 'human' as a kind of rustic recycling that can involve not just objects and plants but whole fragments of landscape. In such

a context, landscape art often blurs quite deliberately any line between spontaneous and shaped effects, so that you cannot tell just where the human hand has begun its work. The juxtapositions that Edith Wharton warned might seem 'monotonous' in Italian villa gardens, essentially monochrome but intense, are often transformed today into a fascinating modern minimalism.

OPPPOSITE For this aromatic parterre at Mas Vincent in Provence, designer Michel Semini and owner Pierre Bergé took inspiration from formal Parisian models, as much for wit and pleasure as for symmetry. The outside landscape disappears.

ABOVE The simple outlines at La Carmejane in Provence, planned by Michel Biehn and owner Frankie Coxe, set off exceptional buildings and a splendid view, with olive crowns by Marc Nucera as foreground.

ABOVE In the country estate of Altavès in Provence, restored by Emile Garcin, the traditional double plane tree avenue is enhanced by sculpted *Viburnum tinus* in a symphony of greens, greys and beige.

OPPOSITE ABOVE LEFT An elegant oval at La Carmejane in Provence, designed by Frankie Coxe and composed of wild bush thyme and limestone cobbles, sits on an upper terrace where coffee is served. It overlooks cherry trees and patchwork farmland.

OPPOSITE ABOVE RIGHT Under Aleppo pines at Le Clos Pascal in Provence, Nicole de Vésian clipped existing box and viburnums, adding pittosporums and santolinas to create a downhill flow that mixes agricultural, wild and formal elements.

OPPOSITE BELOW Designer Dominique Lafourcade loves bilateral symmetry, but in this bastide garden at the Mas du Baraquet in Provence she has adapted the contours of a formal parterre to the rugged cliff wall. Beyond is the rose garden.

TAPESTRIES

In Homer's epics, women are valued as much for their skill in weaving as for their beauty. Nicole de Vésian had been a famous fabric specialist before settling in the Luberon hills in 1986 (see also pp. 48–53). Half Provençal, she had already planted rosemary and lavender in her gardens in Paris. She began experimenting with hard pruning in her first southern garden, situated on the beach near Saint-Tropez. Seeing the natural mounding created by the wind, she shaped her plants so that they would be at their best on her return after long absences. It was here that she first observed that 'all plants love to know they are being cared for and they happily grow back', here that she started picking up stones from the *garrigue* (see p. 106) to use for mulch. Later on, in her small hilltown garden at La Louve, her tapestries varied in area, composition and height, but were always intimately connected with pale stone, as gravel or pebble paths, rustic walls and sculpture.

It was at La Louve that tapestry plantings became Vésian's hallmark: low-growing, small-scaled, layered mounds and globes. Their evergreen or evergrey assemblages could be enjoyed both from within (touch releasing scent) and from above (upper terraces or house windows). Early English visitors winced at what they saw as 'ruthless pruning' and the lack of any 'wanton growth'.[5] This was a misreading. Vésian did not want control but 'harmonious patterns that still leave room for a touch of fancy'. She encouraged many annuals to self-sow – hollyhocks, poppies, even gaillardia. In 1992, after visiting La Louve, the British garden guru Christopher Lloyd wrote: 'The garden's shapes show a bit of yeast-like fermentation and they are always changing.'[6] Not least from season to season, from green new growth to the palest silvers induced by summer drought.

In her landscape gardens on woodland and meadow sites, Vésian worked directly with elements already present: tree trunks carefully selected for graphic interest, mossy stones and massed undergrowth, sometimes clipped, sometimes loose. At La Louve, her tapestries were newly planted, but most of the species she chose grew spontaneously just outside the garden: viburnum, arbutus, rosemary, thyme, cypress, myrtle, juniper and bay laurel. Her asymmetrical groupings deliberately echoed the hillside opposite in their contours, textures and movement. Her clipped greenery was always

La Louve, Provence | Nicole de Vésian
These views of the kitchen terrace (opposite) and the west terrace seen from an upper storey (below) date from 1990, showing the property in Nicole de Vésian's time, as she made it herself. She composed different plant tapestries for each terrace, experimenting with heights, volumes and angles of vision.

sculptural, in that each plant kept its own character. Her talent lay in their combinations, always harmonious from whatever the angle of vision. Each plant fits into a sequence that leads the eye from plane to plane, from near to far, from the most clipped to the most free-form, in a series of balanced volumes and voids. Never static, and never framed to be seen from one direction only, these compositions invite both walking and sitting, discovery and meditation. As Jean-Marie Rey, a nurseryman friend, said, 'She taught me how to remove and reduce, to equate beauty and simplicity.' There was nothing cerebral about this, however; she loved to touch, smell and feel the plants.[7]

Vésian's protégé, tree sculptor Marc Nucera (see p. 81), continued her tapestry work on vertical surfaces, transforming the cypress hedging of old farm properties into fretwork patterns, saving stands of trees that new owners might otherwise have sacrificed. Like Vésian, Nucera excels in salvage, putting the past to new uses, participating in cycles of change.

La Louve, Provence | Nicole de Vésian
Flat-topped cypresses – pruned after frost burn to encourage side growth – became a Vésian signature (opposite). In all of her gardens, including Trabari (below), Vésian practised graded views to lead the eye from near to far, from garden to landscape.

ABOVE Marc Nucera works with quiet deliberation on 'simple forms and limited differences'. He feels that, as with this cypress hedge at a private *mas* in Provence, each plant, each site, possesses its own energies, its unique history and destiny.

BLACK AND WHITE

Jacqueline Morabito has transformed two sites in the back country of the French Riviera: her glade and grove terraces (see pp. 77–79), and a ruined village overgrown with holm oaks, first discovered on a hike in 1995. After clearing away mountains of brambles, she began pruning the remaining vegetation to open sightlines and emphasize pleasing growth habits. Her clipping never produces tight, static, self-contained volumes but encourages soaring, dynamic shapes that let the trunks of taller trees emerge from waves of shrubbery. Morabito speaks of 'creating order out of wilderness' but also of 'revealing what was hidden'. She has now trained two young gardeners to go beyond, as she puts it, the usual status of gardeners as 'outdoor cleaning women'. She has taught them her reverence for what she calls '*la beauté du geste*'.[8] Often, she feels, just a small, well-timed intervention can transform an ordinary place into something magical. Her plants are thriving under such care.

Like Vésian, Morabito builds on a vernacular heritage. But Vésian makes her strong connections between the domestic and the wild as a kind of bridge between near and far, weaving visual links between her tapestries and the shapes, textures and colours of the hillside beyond. Morabito's larger landscapes are self-contained. Both of her sites blend seamlessly into their surroundings but their main focus lies at their heart, not on the margins. They are like

The Hamlet, French Riviera | Jacqueline Morabito

This vast, sculpted landscape 'makes sublime' the flow of time: stone is built up and crumbling, rock eroding, plants growing, both clipped and free form. There is no romantic opposition here of human culture and rampant nature: both are part of the same, ever-evolving harmony.

giant sculptures, impossible to perceive as a whole from any one point of view. Vésian transformed vernacular village houses into comfortable living spaces, incorporating modern techniques and materials when useful, but leaving a general impression of the traditional idiom. Morabito chose two very different approaches to human habitat: in her olive grove, she transformed a sixteenth-century ruin into a modernist white cube. In her hamlet, the limestone walls combine over and over again, never in quite the same way, with clipped greenery. Her mix of ruins and foliage is not like that of the famous Italian garden Ninfa (see pp. 144–49 and 198–201), where curator Lauro Marchetti sees expansive vegetation and potentially crumbling walls as a symbolic confrontation of 'life' (plants) and 'death' (stone). He maintains balance by containing the former but always in such a way that the work of busy secateurs remains invisible. In Morabito's version, stone is as alive as plants, and human participation is proudly displayed. In her glade and grove garden, the main species are pines, oaks and olives; in her ghost town, she shapes holm oaks, box, myrtles and lentisks. Much of the foliage is scented but flowers, though welcome (wild bulbs for example), are accidental. At Ninfa, roses tumbling over crumbling walls are meant to be admired from a little distance, like a picture, while you stand in the shade of tall trees. In Morabito's hamlet, the holm oaks grow much lower and their canopies form the top level of careful sequences that work vertically as well as horizontally. There is no distance: instead of standing back, you go inside. Each scene, as it flows into the next and as you move through it yourself, provides a new variation on contrasts of open and closed space, sun and shade, light absorption and reflection, tone and texture.

Both of Morabito's sites easily translate into monochrome in strong Mediterranean sunshine. Dan Pearson also observed, this time in southern Spain, that 'it is in the black pool of shade under carob and fig where you want to be in the white-out light'.[9] The upper surface of both olive and holm oak foliage can seem, at some times of day, almost black, the underside almost white. In both her landscape works, Morabito lets white lines everywhere glimmer among the dark greens: stripes of pale limestone make lines and circles that mark the driveway and paths. But there is not here the stark opposition between house and setting imposed by Le Corbusier in his famous Villa Savoie, raised on stilts above purely abstract lawn.[10] Morabito's cube house melts into its green surroundings because her whites are pale and soft, luminescent but not brilliant.

The Grove, French Riviera | Jacqueline Morabito
Morabito's works at both the Grove and the Hamlet invite immersion in a seamless continuity, where buildings blend readily with their surroundings. Her soft, white cube house nestles into its shrubberies. On the roof is a dead vinestock, a striking reminder of the live ones below.

White cube houses in Mediterranean settings can look vernacular and ultramodern at the same time.[11] Architectural historians Jean-François Lejeune and Michelangelo Sabatino note the appeal to Italian Futurists in Capri in the 1920s of 'smooth whitewashed surfaces, unadorned simple volumes and flat roofs'. This 'essentialness of ancient simplicity' offered a contemporary choice for housing without becoming a 'vulgar copy of local folkloric elements'. Modernists were long drawn to this kind of peasant heritage by its basic functionalism, its seeming timelessness and its apparent 'freedom from learned and cultural symbolism'. The same historians note a shift within the modernist movement in the 1930s from craft to machinery, from the vernacular to the industrial, orchestrated, they feel, mainly by representatives from northern Europe. They judge that it led more to uniformity than to the desired universality. The white cube house continues to provide a popular connection between modernism and the vernacular, one that Morabito develops with subtlety.

On Cap Ferrat, near Nice, designer John Rocha imagined a completely different symphony in white, green and black. Here, too, as in Morabito's glade and grove garden, an older house has been transformed into white cubes according to the owner's own conception. In both cases, buildings are surrounded by dense plantings. Both have long narrow pools with dark linings to reflect images and sky. Both carefully integrate minute detailing into the larger scale, using exotic objects – travel souvenirs in both cases – to add variety and complexity. In both cases, house, furniture and garden are part of the same vision, intended for year-round outdoor living. Rocha, however, of Asian and Portuguese descent, chose a small lot on glamorous Cap Ferrat, neatly closed off from the world by a clever vertical layering of walls and hedging; Morabito's large, rustic, inland property has no obvious boundaries. Rocha and his family come for quick breaks from a busy life in Dublin; Morabito lives on the Riviera year round. Existing trees in the Rocha garden included palms, whereas Morabito started mainly from oaks and olives. Rocha's request to his garden advisor Benoît Bourdeau was 'Make me a jungle!' He enjoys rich displays of exotic foliage, such as lotus flowers, in lush contrast to the stark shape of the house. Its white

BELOW At the villa on the French Riviera belonging to fashion designer John Rocha, global design sets off brilliant white architecture against shiny, exotic foliage with elegance and wit, in a self-contained, almost portable landscape. On the roof here, a New Zealand kiwi arbour.

is not milky but brilliant, and catches the shadows of fronds, while tendrils snake across gravel paths. The Rochas finally gave up on a solarium project for the roof (much too hot!) and put in a trellis with New Zealand kiwis – the garden's only food crop – instead. Morabito has as a roof sculpture a giant, gnarled vinestock, partner to the living ones below. She produces wine as well as olive oil and vegetables. Rocha has added surrealist animal sculpture – a life-size cow and dragons – and can hear monkeys from the zoo nearby. Morabito welcomes native wildlife. Rocha's garden is full of fun, while Morabito says, 'My garden fills me with joy.' Rocha, like many international celebrities making holiday homes in the south, was keen to enjoy the benefits of an instant garden; Morabito considers that 'a garden is a school for patience, and patience is one thing you cannot buy'.

The Grove, French Riviera | Jacqueline Morabito

Morabito's extremes of dark and light are constantly modulated by intermediate values. Everything is soft and fluid. She designs minimalist, mobile furniture for indoors as well as out, to place anywhere in the garden she may care to picnic.

6

MATORRAL, MAQUIS AND MEADOW

This is the best kind of landscape art; big and generous physically,

interactive, responsive, sensuous, seasonal, even temporary, even witty!

Martha Kingsbury, Californian artist-gardener working in chaparral landscapes[1]

PAGE 104 AND BELOW Gardened *phrygana* in the Aegean near a house in the OLIAROS development, landscaped by doxiadis+. Below is the hillside it imitates.

Mediterranean flora includes about 10% of all known species, in an area covering roughly 1.5% of the earth's land mass.[2] Particularly rich are the plant systems grouped generically by the biodiversity experts under the Spanish term 'matorral'. These are known locally as *garrigue* and *maquis* in France; *gariga* and *macchia* in Italy; *xerovuni* and *phrygana* in Greece; *matorral* and *tomillares* in Spain; *choresh* or *maquis* in Israel; and *bath'a* throughout the Near East.[3] These more or less open systems range from low-growing subshrubs to taller associations that include trees. They may be dynamic, evolving either towards grassland or encroaching forest; in other cases, weather and soil conditions combined with continuous human usage keep matorral landscapes stable for centuries. Specialists differ from country to country in their definitions and usage of these terms: 'In many places, *maquis* (or *macchia*) is considered as the first major stage in

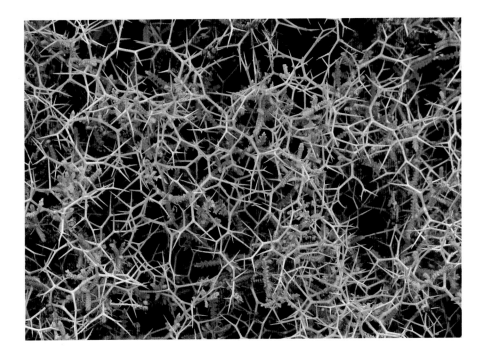

forest or woodland degradation, followed by *garrigue*, *phrygana*, or *bath'a*, which are all of still lower stature and complexity than *maquis*. In France, *garrigues* are said to occur primarily on limestone substrates, while

ABOVE Thorny burnet (*Sarcopoterium spinosum*) growing in the marble quarries of Paros in October. *Phrygana* in Greek means 'friable'. This plant, completely dry and brittle all summer, is just beginning to make its green winter growth.

maquis is reserved for those formations occurring on acid, silicaceous soils.' However they are labelled, these formations fascinate scientists because they present 'a fine-grained mosaic of almost all the growth forms recognized by plant ecologists', from bulb to grass to shrub to tree. April is usually their brightest moment.

Matorral ecosystems have evolved in conjunction with human activity – a combination, say the same experts, of 'thin soils, forest clearance for timber, grazing by livestock, and/or repeated fires'; rarely, however, of actual cultivation. Two thousand years ago the Roman poet Virgil warned prospective farmers against 'the hungry gravel of a hilly country' that 'scarce serves the bees with lowly spurge and rosemary' but could still feed sheep and goats.[4] Virgil's shepherds and their barren settings inspired pastoral art, literature and music for centuries. Today, the natural beauty of sites with 'hungry gravel' draws admirers from all over the world to the Mediterranean. Some hike with backpacks, others build sumptuous secondary residences. Still others worry how such sites may best be preserved, developed and enhanced without upsetting the ecological equilibrium.

AEGEAN *PHRYGANA*

Some six thousand years ago, the islands of the Cyclades already sheltered a distinctive maritime civilization based not on subsistence farming but on the trading of minerals – marble from Paros, obsidian from Melos, pumice from Thera, emery from Naxos, copper and gold from Siphnos, and so on. The sea was not a barrier but a connection to the outside world.[5] Today, the net of commerce is flung even wider. In 2002, Greek developer Iasson Tsakonas returned from Azerbaijan and the US to found OLIAROS, an experimental housing development on the island of Antiparos.[6] Tsakonas assembled a pool of talented young architects to work with landscape architect Thomas Doxiadis, founder of the doxiadis+ agency, and his collaborator for this project, Terpsi Kremali. Their aim was to develop low-density housing harmoniously embedded in a steep, wedge-shaped, matorral-covered piece of hillside. Doxiadis recalls: 'We were all in love with the landscape, wanting to keep it as intact as possible while placing houses which, by Greek standards at

OLIAROS, Antiparos, Greece | doxiadis+
The new, contemporary landscaping blends almost seamlessly with long-existing local ecosystems, which also show variation over short distances. Architects here are deca ARCHITECTURE (above) and tala mikdashi / Maria Doxa (opposite).

least, are large. Each one has a swimming pool, three covered parking spaces and individual exterior driveways. This is a landscape where windswept vegetation stays low. Everything you do shows up immediately. The most important thing was to find an organizing structure for a development visible from so many angles.' The first house was sold in 2005. By 2011, eight houses had been built on about 16 hectares, all adjacent properties with wonderful sea views, but each isolated from its neighbours.

Each house bears the mark of its particular architect but most avoid the generic Cyclades cliché of whitewashed, blue-shuttered cubes. The traditional vocabulary of this particular island is based on houses of only one storey that hug the hillside, built of local stone with flat roofs of rolled earth. Each architect carefully studied the lay of the land for most sensitive placement (one house is half buried). Great care was taken to avoid site destruction during the actual building by providing turning places for heavy machinery on the footprint of the house itself. Excavated earth was recycled to restore the drystone terracing that once supported meagre cultivation on the lower slopes. New building often incorporates vestiges of

older ruins. Within this strikingly beautiful landscape, each small variation has been put to best advantage. The lower reaches are still slightly more lush than the dryer scrubland of the upper parts. There is even a miniature wetland that stays green in summer, called 'pigadakia' ('little wells'), where five small springs surge forth. One of the biggest successes has been the design of the access roads, beautifully incorporated into the contours of the incline so that they are barely visible.

OLIAROS, Antiparos, Greece | doxiadis+
Particular care was taken to integrate roads and paths, immersed in vegetation or hidden behind stone walls. Drystone work was done largely by Albanian masons. Above is a house by deca ARCHITECTURE.

The stonework, largely done here by Albanian builders, is outstanding. The design team has great respect for these craftsmen-artists. Human construction and natural landscape form an exceptionally harmonious whole, whether examined in close detail or admired as broadly framed views onto neighbouring islands. In some parts of Greece, slopes are so steep that there is no middle ground between a house and the sea, but here the incline is gradual enough to allow for a succession of tapestries of varied textures and colours. One of the hillside's most dramatic features is the native juniper locally known as *Juniperus macrocarpa*, or 'snake tree', in homage to its trunks twisted by the prevailing winds.

Preserving local vegetation was a high priority for doxiadis+. Newly planted areas around the houses blend into spontaneous, pre-existing

expanses. Only close inspection reveals a greater concentration, an enrichment and selection of plants in the gardened parts. Thomas Doxiadis explains: 'We started by looking carefully at the way species are organized, their densities and groupings. Nothing is arbitrary. We may plant a drift of A with bits of B, then a drift of B with bits of C, always interlocking. In these linked groupings, what is major in one area becomes minor in the next. At the same time, some parts cleared during the building are left to be colonized by native plants.' Common examples of the latter include *Centaurea spinosa*, *Sarcopoterium spinosum* and a pot marigold, *Calendula arvensis*. The team has begun reproducing some of its own selections.

Most of the hillside is unwatered. In spring, it is one vast colourful floral carpet but in summer, many of these aromatics go dormant and dry out completely. Maintenance is offered as an additional service and most owners take advantage of it, but teams have to be trained. One caretaker painstakingly removed the reviving natural vegetation that was part of the designers' strategy because he thought these plants merely weeds. Another decided that, since it is *phrygana*, it must not need weeding at all. Some owners want plants that grow faster, or flower in summer. The project is a learning experience for everyone, but the results are breathtaking. Doxiadis+ won an Emerging Architecture Awards commendation in 2010 for this project.[7]

OLIAROS, Antiparos, Greece | doxiadis+

Just as plantings melt into *phrygana*, so infinity pools melt into
the Aegean, present all around the promontory. This house is
by tala mikdashi / Maria Doxa.

TUSCAN *MACCHIA*

A stretch of Tuscany's west coast at Argentario has been elaborated along similar principles by landscape architect Paolo Pejrone. Here, too, the project covers a large wedge of steep hillside overlooking the sea. Both sites are large-scaled, and so well integrated that their boundaries are hard to discern. On both, sensitive professionals incorporate large swathes of existing vegetation but enrich it. The Greek version, however, is low-growing scrubland, while the Italian one includes light woodland of oak and pine. Both projects use small ecosystem variations to create different moods that depend on subtle plays on shifting light and shade, open and closed vistas, variations in height and density of planting, contrasts of tone and texture. In both cases, straight lines and sharp angles are used to frame massed mounds and billows. Both experiment with a kind of mini-

malist simplification that is an aesthetic enrichment. Both could only be completed with the help of clients both discerning and affluent.

The Argentario project was begun in 1996. Fifteen of its thirty-five hectares of *macchia* are now gardened, and more will soon be so. Paolo Pejrone (see also pp. 152–55), Italy's most famous contemporary designer, was trained by Russell Page and Roberto Burle Marx. Like both of these pioneers, he combines an architect's fine sense of space with a connoisseur's love of plants. His work is protean in its variety, always adapted to particular sites and clients. In Argentario, he worked closely with architects from Studio Lazzarini Pickering in Rome and especially with the owner, who spends three days a week in his garden following the evolution of its every shoot. Where the landscape of Antiparos mixes

Argentario, Tuscany | Paolo Pejrone

Here, as on the Greek site (pp. 108–13), houses have fine sea views but are themselves hidden from the sea. The Tuscan landscape, however, is layered differently. In Greece, scrubland and strong winds make the plants hug the ground, whereas the Tuscan site is reverting to forest. Undergrowth here includes myrtle, lentisk, phyllirea, buckthorn, viburnum and holm oak.

outcrops of grey rock with the rusts, golds and grey greens of the *phrygana*, the Tuscan property features wood and bare earth more than stone. The dark browns of Tuscan soil, tree trunks and especially of wooden decking here complement the dull greens of holm and cork oaks, arbutus, filarias, laurustinus, bay trees and stone pines – a nuanced palate of local essences. Almost nothing on site was removed but much was added. In both Greece and Italy, the houses are as invisible as possible from the sea, the Tuscan one wrapped in vines and creepers. Particularly striking in the Tuscan garden are crisscrossing perspectives that focus on wooden structures: elegant flights of steps, or the open boxes and low platforms used for seating or outdoor meals. These constructions emerge from the greenery as if airborne, or about to take flight. They are made of chestnut planks first burned to make them almost black, then varnished. This work is done by craftsmen operating in a permanent workshop on the property.

The problems of maintenance are different in each property. The designers in Antiparos try to help clients learn to make their gardens as self-sustaining as possible. In Argentario, under single ownership, eight full-time gardeners work constantly under the direction of the head gardener, Francesco Abbione. A former sailor, he is now delighted to be working in a place where 'gardening means more than just mowing the lawn'. But he also mows the lawn: the Italian site has lush green carpets around the house, spread under olive trees and punctuated with waves of creeping rosemary, although neither of these species

Argentario, Tuscany | Paolo Pejrone
Paths and buildings are not immersed in vegetation here but float above banks of shrubbery, where some specimens grow naturally in mounds, while others need constant pruning.

much appreciates the watering. The main upkeep on the property, however, is pruning: an overall job done three times a year, with touch-ups three days a week. Stonework is done by Romanian immigrants, while Sardinian specialists come every eight years to harvest the cork oaks. In spite of all this organized effort, nothing here seems contrived or strained – not even static. This is an entire, living landscape, with a design that flows and microclimates that provide infinite variety. Migrating birds and other wildlife are welcomed here, too, except for intrusive boars...

Argentario, Tuscany | Paolo Pejrone

Near the house and beyond the elegant pool are swathes of richly watered lawn, in place at the owner's request. Holiday home-owners all over the region enjoy the lush comfort and cool luxury of greenswards in contrast to the surrounding *macchia*, but Mediterranean plants die fast in these conditions.

MEADOW AND MATORRAL

Meadows at first glance seem the opposite of matorral – flat, rich and soft rather than steep, poor and scratchy. Both, however, may be used to feed livestock and both may have a particularly rich flora. Both may be spontaneous, labour-intensive or something in between. Both may be 'old fields'

(abandoned farmland) or the result of deliberate effort by farmers or gardeners. Since the 1990s, there has been in Northern Europe a trend towards meadow gardening, a blending of horticulture and landscape art aiming at more 'naturalistic' moods and practices. Often the great prairies of the American Midwest or the steppes of Germany and Eastern Europe serve as a model. Such subtly managed, idealized countryside is a modern variant on the old pastoral tradition.

It was in fact Mediterranean meadows that first fed this ideal. The Homeric Hymns (c. 700 BC) recount how Demeter's daughter Persephone was abducted while 'gathering flowers over a soft meadow, roses and crocuses and beautiful violets, irises also and hyacinths and the narcissus, which Earth made to grow at the will of Zeus'. Farmers paid the price, however, when Persephone was abducted and Demeter 'caused a most dreadful and cruel year for mankind over the all-nourishing earth'. When Persephone returned, 'springtime waxed, the earth was soon waving with long ears of corn'. In the ancient Greek narrative, flowers and food are as inseparable as mother and daughter. There is no distinction between the human and the wild. All forms of life participate in the energies of fertility and all are equally subject to divine caprice.[8]

Meadows today in Mediterranean Europe are usually abandoned farmland. The biodiversity experts estimate that 'there are between 1,500 and 2,500 species of annuals, biennials, and bulbous plant species in the Mediterranean flora that mostly occur in early stages of succession in cultivated, fallowed, or abandoned fields, terraces, or pastures'.[9] Such sites often take northerners by surprise. Lady Fortescue, settling

ABOVE In April, meadows in Greece produce scented flowers, which, say the Homeric Hymns, 'Earth made to grow to please the Host of Many'. In early summer, drier slopes bloom with subshrubs, like this *Phlomis fruticosa* at the Rou Estate in Corfu.

on the French Riviera in the 1930s, recalls: 'In the autumn we had laboriously planted thousands of bulbs imported, expensively, from Holland. These we planted under the scornful eye of Hilaire [the gardener], who refused to be interested in them – we wondered why. When spring burst upon us one perfect morning (nothing comes gradually in Provence), I found the grassy terraces under the olive-trees one sheet of tiny blue Roman hyacinths, miniature scarlet tulips, mauve and scarlet anemones, and yellow jonquils. When I exclaimed in delight to Hilaire that our predecessor here had planted lavishly and beautifully, he at first looked blank, and then, when I pointed rapturously to the jewelled grass on the terraces below, he gave it one contemptuous glance and said, "*Ah ça! – sont sauvages, Madame.*"[10]

Professional designers in the northern Mediterranean are often asked to provide 'naturalistic' meadows in tune with current fashion. Paolo Pejrone remembers an Iranian client in Italy who 'wanted daffodils, the blue camassia, wild carrots, grasses, and many, many poppies, which will grow only on loose soil. In practice, this meant redoing the field almost daily. I struggled for five years to get a flowery meadow that lasted a month.' Many owners, not all northerners, want meadows in high summer! Greek gardener and writer Cali Doxiadis notes that wild native grasses in Corfu first appear after the October rains, studded with autumn crocuses, cyclamen and, later, wild narcissi. They grow in height and beauty until setting seed, along with their wildflowers, through April. By late May, 'most are rapidly turning into unsightly tussocks of hay, collecting windblown debris, often beaten down'. With summer heat, they become a fire hazard. Imported garden grasses, she claims, fare no better in this climate.[11]

Matorral and meadow both turn golden, brown and sere in Mediterranean summers. Many bulbs, perennials and subshrubs go dormant at that time. This kind of landscape has its own austere beauty. In France, nurseryman Olivier Filippi promotes and illustrates (in his garden and books) an approach to gardening modelled on matorral that is floral in spring, drought-tolerant in summer, good-looking and low-maintenance year round. He and his wife Clara

ABOVE Later in the summer, still in the wild, *Phlomis fruticosa* and similar species produce beautiful seed heads, as here in natural meadows at the Rou Estate in Corfu. Near inhabited areas, sere meadows are often mown for fire prevention.

explore ecosystems all over the Mediterranean, studying those in long-term equilibrium, noting natural associations and necessary growing conditions, reflecting seriously on the migration of plant populations. Their proposals are adaptable to plots of all sizes. They know that the best landscape art – from home garden to whole hillside – sets human energies in tune with seasonal logic and natural law, even though the gods may be as capricious as ever. The invention of summer for holiday-makers is one of the worst misadventures to befall Mediterranean landscapes. Let those who want lush visions of pastoral come south in April, when, as Columella put it, 'all the thousand-coloured flowers are brought forth by bounteous nature[...] Everywhere is fun and wine and care-free laughter; feasts are at their height in joyous meads.'[12] Each season in turn has its beauties: the changes they bring link ephemeral pleasures to ancient experience of cyclical time.

FAR LEFT, LEFT AND ABOVE Wildflowers in the meadows of olive terraces at Bramafam, Piedmont, in October: common mallow (*Malva sylvestris*); mullein (*Verbascum sp.*) among crown vetch (*Coronilla varia*); and the common prickly pear (*Opuntia sp.*).

Mèze, Languedoc | Olivier and Clara Filippi

A beautiful tapestry of drought-tolerant, spring-flowering plants, including *Limoniastrum monopetalum, Tanacetum densum subsp. amani, Artemisia lanata, Centaurea bella, Euphorbia characias subsp. wulfenii* and *Anthyllis barba-jovis.*

FIELD GEOMETRIES

The vines are planted from end to end of the wintry horizon

in regular symmetrical lines, as if on a chessboard...

Lawrence Durrell, *Spirit of Place*, 1969[1]

PAGE 124 On an ancient site at Puglia in Italy, Fernando Caruncho designed a vineyard in the form of a 'Storia come un'onda', or 'history like a wave'.

ABOVE The bastide property of Mas du Baraquet in Provence overlooks broad fields that are part of the estate. The designer, Dominique Lafourcade, planted a swathe of lavender as foreground for crops that may be, from year to year, hay, wheat, sorghum or sunflowers.

The Mediterranean mosaic of working landscapes has been admired for its beauty at least since the first century AD, when Pliny the Younger designed his villa windows to frame it: 'The landscape affords plenty of variety, the view in some places being closed in by woods, in others extending over broad meadows.'[2] Early eighteenth-century Englishmen, says British historian Tim Richardson, considered such country-side to be the 'prime attraction of Italy, above painting, sculpture, archi-tecture'. He cites Joseph Addison in *The Spectator* in 1712: 'One finds something more particular in the Face of the Country, and more asto-nishing in the Works of Nature, than can be met with in any other Part of Europe.' Addison particularly admired Capri, 'cover'd with Vines, Figs, Oranges, Almonds, Olives, Myrtles and Fields of Corn which look extremely fresh and beautiful, and make up the most delightful little Landscip imaginable'.[3]

The extent to which such patterning is regular varies according to period and place. Dividing land into segments, determining where and how the soil is worked, who does the actual tilling and for whose benefit – these are founding acts in any human society and inevitably involve a distribution of power. Roman surveyors are credited with imposing 'the first scientific, i.e., deliberately methodical system of land use in western civilization'.[4] Their tripartite division of countryside into *ager*, *saltus* and *silva* (field, scrub or pasture, and woodland) was organized in part thanks to long aqueducts and highways proudly built straight across country, whatever the obstacles and however varied the topography. In his history of the French landscape, Jean-Robert Pitte judges that the Roman conquest of Gaul, followed by the surveying of the countryside into regular sections, 'engendered for several centuries a homogenization of the landscape that was not seen again until the industrial revolution'.[5] And yet, as the biodiversity experts point out, efficient Roman imperialism worked 'at the scale of a single farm holding' so that, 'for each of the different crops in use, specific landscape units were identified as being the best suited. Therefore, plot limits often coincided with geomorphologic limits.'[6]

Not so for the industrial agriculture practised after World War II, with its vast expanses of a single crop, all plots sown and harvested at the same time regardless of local variations. These uniform tracts can be very photogenic, especially from the air. Their yields are transported on extensive motorways and railroads that admit no impediments. Only in recent years has there been any attempt to adapt these lines of communication to 'geomorphologic limits'.[7] In the 1960s, when hedges in some parts of Europe were uprooted and fields regrouped for machine cultivation, Field Art was invented, also requiring large tracts planted with one or two species.[8] Many field artists promoted aerial views as a means of breaking with classical perspective and the conventions of representation, deliberately rejecting decorative detailing and any utilitarian connection with productivity. These were the years when British

BELOW Drystone walls protect small fields from grazing sheep near Campo in Mallorca. The typical small-scaled Mediterranean patchwork uses geometry to insure diversity, not uniformity. Livestock, tree crops and annuals all play a role.

novelist John Berger, living in a French mountain village, wrote: 'The world is leaving the earth behind.'[9] Never more than from an airplane.

The deliberate rootlessness of those decades seems to have lost its appeal. Today, another kind of rootlessness shapes Mediterranean farmland, sometimes with happier long-term effects. Pliny's cosmopolitan descendants, urban escapees from London or Frankfurt, Sydney or Singapore, are transforming old farmhouses and sheepfolds to set up 'hobby farms', where estate-grown wine and olive oil are a source of great pride. At the same time commercial producers, especially vintners, have discovered landscaping and gardens as marketing attractions. Owners of these contemporary Mediterranean *fermes ornées* (a genre popular also in Australia and California) sometimes engage top landscape designers – Jean Mus, Dominique Lafourcade and Michel Semini in southern France, for example – to link house, garden and fields with an elegance and charm that Pliny would have appreciated. One of the most original practitioners of this genre is the Spanish landscape architect Fernando Caruncho.

BELOW The Lafourcade family gentrifies old farmsteads, here at Les Confines in Provence, by imposing symmetry on both architecture and garden. However, the formality of these *fermes ornées* is adjusted to site and climate for year-round pleasure, not showcase display.

OPPOSITE Field patterns southeast of Rome – a palimpsest of shifting land-uses going back for many centuries. Ancient Roman surveyors imposed such a blending of *ager* (field), *saltus* (scrub or pasture) and *silva* (woodland) all over the Empire.

CLASSICAL CLARITY

By the late eighteenth century, many northerners viewed geometry as the tool of Man oppressing Nature, which, as philosopher Jean-Jacques Rousseau insisted, 'never uses a plumb line'.[10] Curves were natural and 'free', right angles shunned as symbols of domination. Still today, buildings and paths embarrass 'naturalistic' designers who prefer to disguise any human presence. But for those of a 'humanistic' bent, the habitat and trails of our species are as justified in the landscape as those of any other. Fernando Caruncho claims that: 'We live inside nature and are part of its cycles...' There is no contradiction for him then in claiming that 'geometry is the starting point; it's the point of reference for all Gardens, even the most natural'.[11] Long, straight axes and right angles are essential to Caruncho's vision, in which elegant architecture plays an important role. He often takes inspiration not from wilderness (imaginary or artificially contrived) but from down-to-earth agriculture – from field patterns.

Caruncho's work harks back to ancient Greek concepts of what is natural. He experiences geometry as 'the first language', 'the science that helps us to

measure the Earth and to know space'. This Mediterranean sense of form, both intellectual and material, has long been associated with the sculptural quality of southern light. Caruncho's bold, beautifully proportioned blocks of a single species of plant, lawn, bare earth or mineral surfacing live by light. Stretches of still water add reflections, in every sense. For Caruncho, 'light is the most important element... It is also about scale and proportion and the relationship of land and plants to sky...'[12]

Sa Vina Vella, Mallorca | Fernando Caruncho
The lake pavilion, focal point for long green avenues outlining blocks of trees (opposite); the *Pistacia lentiscus* parterre (left); cypress avenues framing distant landscape features (above).

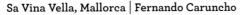

Sa Vina Vella, Mallorca | Fernando Caruncho

The beauty of classical form by no means excludes sensuous pleasures. Colour for Caruncho is not the opposite of form but its necessary complement. Festive evenings (above); intimate patios (opposite).

The project Sa Vina Vella in Mallorca evolved in collaboration with Caruncho's friend, the architect Pablo Carvajal Urquijo, for the latter's own use and, today, for the Cotoner family. Carvajal designed a contemporary interpretation of a vernacular farmhouse as a weekend residence often used for entertaining. Caruncho surrounded it with a grid of sixteen large squares, each containing a single, characteristically Mediterranean species (pomegranates, palms, etc.). Hedges of clipped oleanders and lines of alternating olive and cypress trees frame the compositions. In front of the house is an artificial lake, a vast mirror edged with the same local stone used for the house foundations. Extending into the lake is a pavilion or summer house, inspired by Swedish architect Gunnar Asplund's Woodland Chapel (1918–20). An expanse of water is not incongruous in this region of richly irrigated farmland. Its biomorphic forms echo the crests of mountains on the horizon. More flowing curves connect house and lake in a grand parterre of lentisk (*Pistacia lentiscus*). This species is common locally in the wild, but here it has been clipped into waves. Outside of this central composition, formal wheat fields are flanked by sloping wildflower meadows. As you walk through the garden, you discover that its long, straight axes direct the eye towards distant features – the towers of the local village or of the architect's family estate next door. The main viewpoint is from a broad loggia running the whole length of the southern façade of the house, spectacular when lit up at night. Every detail here adapts vernacular resources to new uses. Techniques and materials are both traditional and modern. Both gardener and architect are deeply rooted locally but operate globally.

Sa Vina Vella was one of Caruncho's early works, like the famous Mas de les Voltès, which also contrasts wheat fields and vineyards, olives and cypresses – all Mediterranean icons. Caruncho has since moved on to experimenting with circles as well as grid patterns. Such meditations are, however, never merely abstract or conceptual – no more than are the courtyards and gardens of Andalusia, which provided his early aesthetic education. Caruncho prefers to be called a 'gardener' rather than 'designer' and considers that, 'as our civilization loses its contact with agriculture, it loses in turn the natural rhythms and traditions imposed by the seasons; the garden also offers a means of renewing contact with these natural cycles'.

At the ancient site of Amastuola in Puglia, southern Italy, Caruncho recently designed a hundred-hectare vineyard called 'La Storia come un'onda' ('history like a wave'). Past layers of time, productivity and beauty are here combined in modern geometries, framed again by venerable olive and cypress trees.

Sa Vina Vella, Mallorca | Fernando Caruncho

The lake pavilion, or summer house, with its copper roof (opposite above) is directly opposite the main farmhouse. Both are at once very contemporary and inspired by much older models.

Sa Vina Vella, Mallorca | Fernando Caruncho

Blocks of single species in staggered rows (*Phoenix canariensis*, opposite below) are outlined with avenues of cypresses and olive trees. Ample water makes green grass (above) a viable part of the pattern.

SOFT MINIMALISM

Renaissance philosopher Michel de Montaigne condemned northern French garden architecture as an 'unbending system' and commended the Italians who 'borrow an infinity of graces, not known among us, from the very irregularity of surface'.[13] Uneven southern topography provides from the start a diversity of viewpoints, further enhanced by the traditional interpenetration of house and garden. In Fernando Caruncho's studio in Madrid, a watchtower, the site's highest point, offers the broadest vista as well as a place for meditation close to the celestial vault. His courtyard gardens show a similar Islamic influence: completely enclosed landwards, open only to the sky, but with a horizontal prospect from the roof terraces. In such a case, between heaven and the horizon, there is little visible middle ground.

Sa Vina Vella has its loggia offering a plunging view onto the formal designs below. But there Caruncho also practises graded views, more or less horizontal, moving harmoniously from near to far, from intimacy to panorama, making use of all the site's irregularities to create

BELOW Alain David Idoux's triangular lavender field at the Mas de Benoît in Provence, with rows converging on a stone obelisk. As one walks past, the distant view shifts from mountains to hilltown. The whole field is kinetic sculpture.

variety. In Provence, Nicole de Vésian refined this progression to an unusual degree, as did two younger artists she influenced, Alain David Idoux and Marc Nucera (see pp. 80 ff.). All three played, for example, with fields of lavender. Vésian made a small-scaled tapestry, alternating globes and fountain shapes (clipped and unclipped plants), to be seen from the terrace just above. Nucera designed a sunken patio in the middle of a long strip of lavender running through a meadow. Idoux's lavender field at the Mas de Benoît is a wedge rather than a rectangle, its apex marked by a stone obelisk in line with jagged hilltops and a medieval village beyond. The balance changes step by step as you walk along the base of the triangle, a kinetic perspective. All three artists excel at balancing shapes, planes, volumes, textures and colours from near to far. Their work never imposes abstract form on site irregularities, still less symmetry. It always includes, indeed highlights, existing characteristics and vegetation.

Like the houses in Vésian's gardens, the farmstead at the Mas de Benoît was rebuilt on the vernacular model (here by the architect Hugues Bosc). It is vaguely central, by no means hidden, but does not in any way dominate its surroundings. Graded views start already from the living-room couch, move through carefully placed windows, and continue to the medieval hill town and silver line of the Alpilles hills on the horizon. In between, in a circle around the house, Idoux created a series of landscape works of which the lavender field is only one, all occupying the middle ground. They all blend so successfully with the setting that conventional visitors sometimes ask, 'But where is the garden?' Idoux also refused to impose any itinerary or even to suggest a sequence with paths or hedges. The whole composition is like a loose labyrinth where crossing perspectives reveal new discoveries whichever way you go. Rough grassland

ABOVE RIGHT Marc Nucera's lavender field at Mas de Michel in Provence leads the eye to a blue tree, then beyond. The sunken patio, with its wood and pebble stools, is invisible from any distance.

RIGHT At La Louve in Provence, Nicole de Vésian planted a tiny lavender field to be seen from above and within. She experimented with different tapestry patterns, juxtaposing clipped with unclipped and rounded with fountain-shaped plants allowed to flower.

Mas de Benoît, Provence | Alain David Idoux

Stone lines: a spiral links almond trees (above) and a serpentine trail leads to a stone cross (opposite). Minimalism here is not abstraction but a distillation of natural energies with implicit spiritual symbolism.

(flower-starred much of the year) links the parts. There are occasional almond trees, remnants of former cultivation, sculpted by Marc Nucera and now Guillaume Laguna. In one place, an almond plantation has been reshaped in the form of a giant spiral underscored by a line of white limestone. Elsewhere a dry stone and cactus 'river' leads to another obelisk, rising against the mountains. These are not controlled 'pictures' but works that invite meandering.

Idoux also learned from Vésian to weave together *ager*, *saltus* and *silva* on one site. The scale here is entirely Idoux's, however; there is lots of breathing space. Geometry sits lightly, the lines remain a little rough. The stone and almond spiral is rustic and irregular, set off by drifts of wild orchids. In the olive avenue, each tree is an individual as it rises from its ring of santolina. Unity comes from the limited range of materials, always local, always soft in tone and coarse in texture – wood, stone, grassland and the evergreen foliage of ordinary species. Nothing is mannered or extravagant. Hardscape and plantings are equally organic, of the earth. It is easy to believe at the Mas de Benoît the claim of the French philosopher Roger Caillois that art is 'merely a particular case of nature'.[14]

Water is not a feature at the Mas de Benoît. The very dryness of the land is part of its austere beauty. But the area around the house has lush lawn, a strong contrast with fields that turn sere as the year advances. Lawn usually belongs to northern climates not only because it needs water but also because it shows to best advantage in broad spaces open to the sky. Such sites in the Mediterranean are used for agriculture while gardens are usually tucked around a house, shaded in summer by green roofs – pergolas, trellising or canopies of deciduous foliage. Outdoor living spaces are intimate and sequential, very different from the open stretches of the north.

Broad expanses of lawn in Mediterranean properties have always had English connotations. Edith Wharton wrote with regret in 1904 about the 'Britannic craving for a lawn' which was replacing olive orchards and vineyards around Italian villas in her day. It was not a new phenomenon even then. When Lord Brougham first settled on the French Riviera in 1834, he and his friends 'astounded the inhabitants of Cannes by their immense, ever-green lawns'.[15] In those days, the British imported turf by boat in the autumn, enjoyed it through the winter and abandoned it in summer, when the lawns became as bare, says an Englishwoman in 1927, as a

ploughed field.[16] Fernando Caruncho in fact incorporates squares of brown, ploughed earth in his gardens, but for winter, not summer effects. In June, these plots become golden, windblown wheat fields, juxtaposed with … swathes of green lawn. Brown, green and soft gold are equally beautiful and important for Caruncho's overall formal patterning as it evolves through the seasons. His use of lawn makes sense on wetlands or amid irrigated farmlands, where water is plentiful. Less sensitive designers use it in more controversial ways. Lawn, say researchers tracing its history, is generally objectionable because of its 'toxicity, habitat destruction, resource depletion, and enforced conformity'.[17] Nothing could be further from the Mediterranean sense of local diversity and logic of place.

'The core of Mediterranean history,' write the historians Horden and Purcell, 'is the control and harmonization of chaotic variability.'[18] Harmonization, but not homogenization: this definition embraces, among other things, the region's patchwork agriculture. The works of Fernando Caruncho and Alain David Idoux show that geometry in landscape art does not mean abstraction, no more than it necessarily imposes a separation between earth and sky. Geometry may rather be a process of distillation, the removal of the superfluous, a kind of simplification that blends intellectual with sensuous pleasure while remaining immediately rooted in specific sites and places.

Mas de Benoît, Provence | Alain David Idoux
Wild grass (opposite and below left), lush in spring and autumn, is supplemented by lines of pennisetum that accompany a path. This axis is flanked first by formally shaped holm oaks (*Quercus ilex*), later by olive trees.

Mas de Benoît, Provence | Alain David Idoux
Close to the house (below), the owners chose to establish lush lawn, watered all summer, when the rest of the property turns golden.

GARDEN

This is gardening that provides useful ornament for our household, numerous species of root, herb, flower and fruit with many marvels.

Olivier de Serres, *Théâtre d'Agriculture et mesnages des champs*, 1600[1]

PAGE 142 An elegant, contemporary version of the 'grandmother's garden' at Mireille Ferrari's Domaine de la Malherbe on the French Riviera: small, dense, plant-heavy, very personal, showing a deep knowledge of local and seasonal growing conditions.

ABOVE Hanbury Botanical Gardens at La Mortola, Italy, begun in 1867 by an English tea merchant returned from China. His extraordinary collection, enriched by later generations, constitutes one of the world's greatest botanical gardens. From the start, it featured useful as well as ornamental species.

OPPOSITE BELOW LEFT In this vegetable garden, southeast of Rome, each small salad gets complete attention. Paolo Pejrone, a hands-in-the-dirt designer, recalls that the Bible names gardening as the world's oldest profession: 'The Lord God took the man and put him in the garden of Eden to till it and keep it' (Genesis 2:15).

What is a Mediterranean garden? One British expatriate in Spain protested: 'Just a courtyard with a trellis, some pots and a few fruit trees, they call that a garden!' This is in fact a good summary of the vernacular garden: snuggled close to living spaces, planned for private family enjoyment but convivial, organized to keep out extremes of weather and maintain even temperatures year round, consuming little energy other than manpower, combining flowers and fruit, pleasure and productivity, a garden for frugal good living in all seasons. Historians of ancient Mediterranean civilizations offer a more ambitious but complementary definition: 'The garden, whether it be an orchard, a place to grow vegetables, a temple or palace courtyard or a private retreat, is a clearly defined space where highly developed skills are used in the service of an ideal.'[2] They warn modern readers that ancient Mediterranean usage, from Assyria and Egypt to Rome, from peasant hovel to palace, made no distinction between ornamental and productive gardening. The warning is necessary because Northern European cultures have effectively separated the two. Since the Renaissance, it has been felt that beauty should be aloof from vulgar necessity. And yet our Western visions of paradise are all Mediterranean, from the Biblical Eden and Homer's palaces to early Persian and Islamic interpretations. And in all of them, fruit counts as much as or more than flowers.

In vernacular gardens all over the world, beauty is simply one pleasure among many, the eye just one of the senses gratified by growing plants. The practical uses of gardening go far beyond the merely edible or even medicinal. The Roman poet-agronomist Columella recommended the *hortus numerosus*, the multiple garden, infinitely variable in content and in function. Nor was this merely a private phenomenon. The historians Horden and Purcell judge that 'the Mediterranean garden is a more typical image of primary production than the wheat field or the grazed hillside. Diversity of labour, technique or intensity, as well as of the quality and quantity of what is tended on the small scale, are structural features of Mediterranean history.'[3] Wealth might be measured not only by the number of species but also by the range of practical uses that could be discovered for a single one, such as the date palm or the olive. Gardeners of all means and conditions collected, propagated, traded. The biodiversity experts recall that 'not so long ago, a huge range of Mediterranean fruit, nut, herb, and also fodder plant varieties were propagated, cultivated, and continually "improved", according to the needs and tastes of growers and consumers. Over the centuries, hundreds of varieties of olive, almond, pear, pomegranate, wheat, barley, alfalfa, and grape, etc., were passed down and preserved *in hortus*.' They cite 382 named cultivars of almond once grown on the island of Mallorca alone.[4] Nineteenth-century markets in Basra offered 360 types of date. The countryside that produced such diversity was itself cultivated like a big garden. This was the *coltura mista* that Fernand Braudel so admired in Morocco, Algiers and the Po valley[5] and that is still inspiring enlightened developers today (see p. 210).

(see p. 210).

BELOW AND BOTTOM RIGHT Private gardens in Corfu and Corsica. The traditional vernacular courtyard, snuggled against the house, with its pots and fruit trees, is transformed today into a main feature for designer gardens, much appreciated for dining in the cool of the evening.

ANGLO-ITALIAN

Italy offers a unique mix of the ancient and the international in its garden heritage. Cultural hybridization began with the Romans, then peaked again in the eighteenth century with the Grand Tour. Since 1800, French and English influences have almost overpowered local talent, so much so that even now most Italian professionals train outside the country and new work in Italy is often done by foreigners. The most admired modern Italian garden today is surely Ninfa, south of Rome, global for centuries and yet local to the point of being, in today's jargon, deeply 'site-generated'.

Pliny the Elder describes a sacred spring consecrated to the Nymphs in the first century AD on what was probably this site. Later a thriving medieval town, it belonged to the Caetani family from 1297 to 1977. Three generations of Caetanis and their English or American spouses transformed Ninfa, beginning in the 1920s, into a legendary garden. Today, owned by the Roffredo Caetani Foundation, the property is lovingly managed by Lauro Marchetti, former protégé and friend of the last Caetani gardener, Princess Lelia. It is hardly a vernacular venture: the Caetanis were princes, popes and ambassadors. Nor is it obviously Italian: Ninfa's website describes it as an 'English romantic garden'. Lelia clearly looked to England for her models and often her sources. The author Charles Quest-Ritson claimed that 'Ninfa could only have been made by English owners', but in a later book he came to value the Italian contribution.[6]

Ninfa, Lazio | Caetani family
Three views of Ninfa's legendary streams and lake. The Roman bridge (below); the Ponte del Macello (opposite above); and the gardens and castle from the hillside above (opposite below).

Ninfa, Lazio | Caetani family

The men associated with Ninfa – the Caetani brothers Gelasio and Roffredo, Lelia Caetani's husband Hubert Howard, their son Esme, and curator Lauro Marchetti – have all valued fruit (such as pomegranates, left), farming and the environment as well as ornamental display. Their ideal owes as much to Virgil as to the Romantics.

What, specifically, is English about Ninfa? Quest-Ritson claims that 'Englishmen believe that a garden is primarily a place to grow plants' – meaning, of course, ornamentals. Each generation at Ninfa collected hundreds of horticultural treasures, selected mainly for their flowers. In spring today, 1,300 varieties of trees and shrubs are in bloom: magnolias, ornamental cherries and crab apples, dogwoods, tulip trees, viburnums, ceanothus and roses, a Ninfa speciality. Bulbs and wildflowers self-sow – anemones, cyclamen, marguerites, primulas among them. Is plant collecting specifically English? Helena Attlee, another respected garden historian,[7] records centuries of Italian examples in private and public gardens, largely unacknowledged by expatriate English. But, says Quest-Ritson, these were 'botanical' rather than 'horticultural' – a distinction hard to pin down. One consideration is that botanical gardens, a genre first invented in Italy, were always concerned with multiple plant uses, not only with beauty and rarity. Today, of the approximately one hundred botanical gardens and arboreta on the Mediterranean rim, forty-two are in Italy.[8]

Princess Lelia, a keen painter, also espoused at Ninfa the English notion of a garden as a series of pictures, impressionist in style, featuring dabs rather than lines. In the 1920s, Gelasio Caetani had planted a majestic cypress avenue along the original Roman road; later this axis was allowed to become blurred, superimposed with curving paths in the Romantic mode. Today, Charles Quest-Ritson remarks, 'Ninfa is a garden almost without structure.'[9] English designer Russell Page, who often worked in Italy in the same years, considered that the use of dabs without lines was liable to produce gardens that would offer a 'series of charming incidents beautifully gardened but incoherent and unrelated to the site'. He cited as an example the Royal Horticultural Society gardens at Wisley, as they then were.[10]

Ninfa, Lazio | Caetani family

The seventeenth-century *hortus conclusus* within the castle walls contains a large water reserve and lush orchards, also beautiful but with a different mood.

What saves Ninfa from this fate is precisely its site, unique and magical, which all of its gardeners have lovingly enhanced. Ninfa's abundant springs surge forth where the alluvial Pontine plain meets the limestone Lepini hills: they create special growing conditions that allow birch to thrive along with tropical fruit, copper beech with holm oaks. The ruins of Ninfa are also distinctive. The architectural historian Geoffrey Scott, a key figure in the 1900 Anglo-Italian Tuscan revival, complained that 'the habit of smothering fine architecture in vegetation is peculiarly English'.[11] Here, however, the ruins are remarkable precisely because of their union with cascading plants. They also form a magic circle, invisible from outside, so that entering the garden is like changing dimensions. And yet, however 'unearthly' and 'dreamlike' Ninfa may be, however English its plantings, the vernacular Italian landscapes rise everywhere beyond the walls, visible from all over the garden, a significant part of its moods. So much so that, already in the 1950s, Hubert Howard (Princess Lelia's husband) began a struggle to preserve them. Many battles later, in 2010, the Foundation inaugurated a wildlife conservation area covering about 100 hectares of the 'wildlife habitats that typified the Pontine Plain before industrial and urban development'.[12] Ninfa also manages successful farms, quite separate from the gardens; their organic produce sells out fast in local markets. The greater Ninfa today takes good care of *hortus*, *saltus* and *ager*, but, in the English mode, keeps them apart. What links all three, however, is Ninfa's magical, protean water, which makes no distinction between use and beauty.

Ninfa, Lazio | Caetani family

A tower links the lush gardens to the austere hillside beyond (opposite left). Outside Ninfa's walls (opposite right), the remains of a wicker plantation (*Salix viminalis*): Lelia Caetani removed weeping willows in the main gardens. *Gunnera manicata* near the wooden bridge (above). Water plants thrive in this pure and constantly moving stream (right).

DESIGNER ITALIAN

In 1994, Paolo Pejrone – the leading Italian landscape architect (see also pp. 114–19), plant collector and columnist for *La Stampa* – began to make a garden for himself in the hills of his native Piedmont at Bramafam, a semi-fortified domain of almost 5 hectares on a steep hillside at 400 metres altitude. Although relatively recent, it has much in common with Ninfa, starting with rich collections of ornamental flowering shrubs and trees: arbutus, magnolias, azaleas, philadelphus, cornus, hydrangeas and roses. As at Ninfa, cascades of flowers obscure structure and line, in this case crumbling stone wall terracing. Carpets of bulbs emerge from spreading ground covers: snowdrops, cyclamens and muscaris, later to be covered with ferns. Pejrone calls Bramafam a 'wild' garden, though it is also his laboratory. Like Lauro Marchetti, he practises purely organic methods, encourages self-sowing and welcomes wildlife. Bramafam is also a world of its own surrounded by mountains, although the plains it overlooks have turned into industrial landscapes. At Bramafam, as at Ninfa, only plants that suit local conditions are retained. But this site also offers many microclimates, so Pejrone can experiment with gunnera and bamboos in the gulch, with Mediterranean holm oaks and cistus in a protected lower corner. Italian Vice President of the International Dendrology Society, counting among his clients the powerful and the princely of today's Italy, Pejrone knows all about cosmopolitan garden style. However, unlike the Caetanis, he has had no qualms about combining productive and ornamental plantings. He regularly includes fruit trees and often potagers in his clients' gardens; he loves equally the *Davidia* and the persimmon. Bramafam contains thirty varieties of fig and vast terraces of productive olive trees emerging from wild flower meadows above the oceans of dogwoods and magnolias. Another major difference: although this is not a graphic or architectural garden, neither is it painterly (organized as a series of pictures). Bramafam requires immersion, the kind that lets you discover small, simple things, such as the wild strawberries that have settled spontaneously along many paths. Its scenes are never isolated from smell and touch. They do not make you stand back but enclose you, the better for you to enjoy their subtle changes from season to season.

Bramafam, Piedmont | Paolo Pejrone

Parts of this property date back to the fourteenth century. The owner, Paolo Pejrone, attributes his love of gardening to his grandmother and a peasant couple who first taught him to grow vegetables, raise chickens and propagate plants.

Bramafam, Piedmont | Paolo Pejrone

Bramafam has many microclimates but is also experiencing global warming. Halfway up the slope, old European oaks (*Quercus robur*) rise among collections of flowering trees and shrubs, including *Davidia involucrata*, hydrangeas and dogwoods (opposite). Oaks and chestnuts are now suffering, but olive trees on the higher terraces thrive among wild iris in the meadows (above). This is a very personal garden for working and living.

MEDITERRANEAN HOMESTYLE

Mireille Ferrari, now in her eighties, has a tiny garden on the French coast between Saint-Tropez and Marseille. As a child she spent holidays on this land, now a protected nature zone. Nearby is the family vineyard, Domaine de la Malherbe, which she directed for years before retiring. Some decades ago, she and her husband built a house right at the point where a narrow stretch of limey beach, almost pure sand, meets the essentially acid and shallow vineyard soil. A limestone crescent facing southwest, the house is half buried in what was once a quarry excavation, its aspect simultaneously contemporary and ancient. House and garden are only visible once you are on the spot, 'a kind of nest' says Madame Ferrari. The main garden area covers only 350 square metres and is spread out on a level with her bedroom on the upper storey. It is internally divided by small stone terraces and plantings that screen hidden corners, so that it seems much larger. There is no main viewpoint or focus but a free flow; even the pruned shrubs are simply curves and billows that slip into tighter globes in key positions. The shaping is never regular or predictable. It barely manages to anchor a space that is all air, light, sand and cloud...

Madame Ferrari is a lover of wild gardening but prunes constantly. She feels that her clipping simply imitates the strong sea winds that trim beach plants into rounded cushions. Moreover, as a vintner, she considers pruning a kind of nurture that keeps plants thriving. In earlier years, she made formal topiary but now prefers looser shapes. Her boxwood lambs have grown to sheep and become a favourite hiding place for big green lizards. Her plant choices are limited by salt sprays, windstorms and sand, and include salt-resistant plants such as dwarf asphodels, the stately silvery *Anthyllis barba-jovis* and the dune lily, *Calystegia soldanella*. Only happy plants remain here, and many spread. But like Lauro Marchetti at Ninfa, Madame Ferrari insists: 'Each plant in my garden is chosen, even if it has sown itself.' She has collected many horticultural varieties of perennials and bulbs, but anything too showy has been banned. One guiding principle has been to use nursery improvements on plants already common in the area, such as junipers and arbutus, myrtles, lentisks, cistus, lavatera and dorycniums (*D. hirsutum* and *D. suffruticosum* syn. *pentaphyllum*), spurges and sedums. She does not insist on native plants; this would hardly be possible in a region where Australian

La Malherbe, French Riviera | Mireille Ferrari
House and garden are inseparable from one another and from the magnificent seascapes beyond. Materials, plants and inspiration come mainly from the location, but the gardener also welcomes outside influences.

acacias have been covering hillsides for decades. Nor is this a collector's garden in the sense of including one of everything. But Madame Ferrari has not lost her sense of wonder at each new variety's unique turn of leaf, nuance of colour, specific growth habit or scent. Textures also mean a lot to her. She has found many unusual uses for weathered wood – beams and shutters of the house, trellising and furniture, decoy ducks with their paint worn off. Her pruning reveals the rough trunks of climbing vines and trees – arbutus, pines and cork oaks in particular. Driftwood from the beach or a dead branch from the mountains (now a perch for birds) echo the gnarled vinestocks of nearby fields. Russell Page, discussing seaside views, recommended using contrasting verticals in the fore and middle ground. Madame Ferrari does this with a striking stand of driftwood, each piece held in place against strong winds by the kind of iron support used in making reinforced concrete.

All three gardens – Ninfa, Bramafam and La Malherbe – are beautifully integrated into surroundings which are themselves part of the experience. Each makes the most of an unusual site, working in harmony with existing elements and conditions. All excel in their attention to fine detail as well as broad vistas, maintaining a harmony of proportions on every scale, although their sites differ greatly in size and topography. All three mix wild gardening and horticultural adventure, with the richest bloom in April, poorest in August, and variety year round. In all, plant connoisseurs have enriched but not excluded existing

La Malherbe, French Riviera | Mireille Ferrari

The main garden (below left and right) at upper-storey level, with its wooden trellis and the clipped crown of the olive tree growing below, seen from two opposite angles. In the spring garden (opposite), wild poppies grow beside topiary sheep.

species. All three use dabs of colour rather than graphic hardscape or strong lines to define space. All three have crisscrossing points of view that play on shifting light, variable from hour to hour and month to month. These effects can only be discovered by walking around, which all these gardeners do, constantly, as often as possible and in all seasons. All three excel in the art that Russell Page described as the 'subtle and deliberate disorder that softens the emphasis of a straight line and never allows the garden to appear static or achieved'.[13]

The Marchettis, Paolo Pejrone and Mireille Ferrari all know every bud and bird of their gardens, which they experience as a place of deep personal significance and as a continuing celebration. All share Paolo Pejrone's opinion that 'the garden is a living creature that would like to be happy. Man must intervene with love, care and a desire to protect.' He adds, 'You go into the garden in the morning and think: I have deserved all this?'[14]

La Malherbe, French Riviera | Mireille Ferrari

Ferrari plays on foliage textures and graded views in changing light, particularly on the Mediterranean continuum from wild to sculpted. A pruned holm oak (opposite); a driftwood stand (left); and rough rock sculptures (above).

SEASCAPES

'It is on this sea that once floated the mysterious news that the great
god Pan was dead. All the oceans of the world have carried the sarcophagi
of saints, but only this one has been touched by words of such power.
On this sea, there is a point, not marked on maps, where Egypt, Judea,
Africa and Provence meet and mingle. There must be a slight tremor,
a Gordian knot, a kind of heart.'

Jean Giono, *La Pierre*, 1955[1]

The Mediterranean came into existence when three continents first pulled apart some 250–200 million years ago.[2] Its present size and shape were fixed 5 million years ago when a series of tectonic shudders broke open the Straits of Gibraltar and let the Atlantic rush in. The biodiversity researchers describe the Mediterranean's northern edge as 'a jagged coastline full of inlets and bays, interior basins and seas such as the Balearic, Adriatic and Aegean', complete with some '11,879 islands and islets, 243 of which harbour permanent human populations'.[3] Where rivers meet the sea and fresh water encounters salt, there are extensive wetlands, deltas, lagoons and salt marshes, just as typical of the region as its arid scrubland.

On sea as on land, Mediterranean peoples have survived by making the most of microclimates linked to topographical fragmentation. Adaptation was always the key. The Greek poet Hesiod, around 700 BC, recommended that farmers work as sailors in the off season. Farmers farmed, hunted, tended flocks, mined, burned charcoal and produced luxury items for market. Seafolk fished, dried salt and traded or raided up and down the coast. Many coastline villages today are still fortified. The relationship between seafront and inland hills has always been ambiguous. Mountains offered refuge but also some measure of isolation, so that indigenous cultures, languages and species survived better inland. Coastal populations could exchange with other civilizations: 'The shores of Greece are like hems stitched on to the lands of barbarian peoples,' said Roman orator Cicero.[4] But coastal wetlands, vulnerable to pirates, also bred disease. In many parts of Europe, sons inherited productive inland pastures while uninhabitable seafronts were left to daughters.

PAGE 162 AND ABOVE Once prosperous but now abandoned hamlets, as at the Rou Estate in Corfu, are often converted into year-round centres for luxury cultural tourism, complete with infinity pools. Designers are becoming more ecologically aware.

LEFT AND OPPOSITE Unique ecosystems created along Mediterranean coastlines by inlets and islands – as at Corsica (left) and Albania, seen from Corfu (opposite) – are today much endangered by summer crowds.

After World War II, this situation was dramatically reversed by the draining and spraying of marshes. Today, as the scientists point out, 'The demand for coastal landscapes for their beauty and tourist attraction makes them particularly vulnerable to unsustainable population increase, especially on the islands. Each summer, the population swells even further, thanks to tourist influxes from around the world. For example, on the French Roussillon coast, it is not uncommon to observe small towns of 10,000 year-round inhabitants swell to 200,000–300,000 during the summer months of July and August, with deleterious impacts on the local surroundings, in terms of contamination, pollution, habitat destruction for plants and animals, and over-exploitation of limited natural resources.'[5]

BELOW Dawn at Porto Vecchio, southern Corsica. Later, this beach may be strewn with picnic garbage. A local fisherman would know at what hour exactly his catch will pass this way.

ABOVE LEFT The life-guard watch-tower at Avlaki Beach in Corfu.

ABOVE Pontikonisi, or Mouse Island, with the white monastery of Vlacherna at sunset.

LEFT The wine-dark Aegean waters.

PLANETARY VISION

The French Conservatoire du Littoral is a government agency founded in 1975 to protect the ecological balance of coastline sites while developing them for public use. Although many of its properties are expanses of natural vegetation, the Conservatoire regards human heritage as an essential part of biodiversity and protects a number of fine gardens. The Domaine du Rayol lies on the French Riviera between Toulon and Saint-Tropez. It is a dynamic experimental site, rich with secret luxuriance and amazing col-

lections, spread over 25 hectares between two rocky headlands. Until the 1890s, this valley was still a mix of woodland and small terraced orchards set among cork oaks and chestnut trees. It was long accessible only by donkey or boat, but in those years a small rail line was built along the coast. In 1909, a banker bought this land to build an elaborate summer home, which after World War I became the Hôtel de la Mer, then the offices of an aeronautics company, and is today the Domaine's main reception building. Other historic vestiges include a smaller Art Deco house with a formal garden, built in 1927 on the eastern promontory, a fisherman's cottage and farm buildings, one of which is now the 'Café des jardiniers'. After World War II, a period of abandonment opened the site to potential speculation. In 1988, it was saved from developers by the Conservatoire.

This one hillside, with its typical Riviera history, combines several characteristic vernacular landscapes, along with a good variety of microclimates and ecosystems. The ecologist Gilles Clément (see also pp. 30–33) was invited here to imagine a project that would encompass this diversity. Clément, who teaches at the school of Landscape Architecture at Versailles, still prefers to be called a gardener. He had long practised an approach to gardening in which humans participate in the natural dynamics of landscape growth. The ravine site at the Rayol is now managed as a Clément-style 'Moving Garden': plants such as stipas are allowed to self-sow and their populations to evolve. Gardeners keep the site from reverting to forest, and prevent any one plant, such as acanthus, from completely eradicating its rivals. When first asked to make

Domaine du Rayol, French Riviera | Gilles Clément

Clément decides with the gardeners how to manage the Rayol's evolving ecosystems. 'Biological reality' comes before good looks, but the result combines both. Coastal views (opposite and right), and the 'Moving Garden' now being colonized by wild acanthus and dwarf fan palms (above).

Domaine du Rayol, French Riviera | Gilles Clément

The farmhouse, now the 'Café des jardiniers' (above), beneath a clump of *Cylindropuntia tunicata*. The Hôtel de la Mer (opposite) is flanked by Canary Island plantings, here considered a Mediterranean ecosystem.

suggestions for the Domaine, Clément was working out his idea of the 'Planetary' garden – the whole earth viewed as a garden with humankind as caretaker. The idea came to him when he first saw the earth photographed from the moon. He proposed to plant a 'Jardin des Méditerranées' ('Garden of many Mediterraneans'). This is not merely a collection of flora from Mediterranean-climate regions round the world, something that other distinguished botanical gardens have already done, but a collection of landscapes, of plant assemblages typical of regions with growing conditions similar to the Rayol's. Each recreated landscape has its own requirements and each has its stars. The Australian 'mallee' shows off banksias, eucalyptus, grevilleas, acacia (fifty species) and callistemon species, as well as 'Kangaroo Paws' (*Anigozanthos*). The subtle colours of New Zealand grasslands set off *Metrosideros*, tea trees (*Leptospermum*), phormiums and a deep shady valley of tree ferns kept moist with artificial mist. The South African 'fynbos' has the densest concentration of species per square metre, many of them very colourful, including *Carissa, Leonitis, Watsonia, Polygala*, amaryllis, pelargoniums, restios, and the King Protea (*Protea cynaroides*) that inspired Clément to make a mosaic by the grand pergola. Chile brings its puyas, its zigzag bamboos (*Chusquea* sp.), its alstroemerias, various nasturtiums (*Tropaeolum* sp.) and cactus candles. The Canary Islands area features echiums and aeoniums, euphorbias and *Dracaena draco*. The Californian garden includes eschscholzias, *Hesperaloe*, yuccas, romneya and ceanothus. Central America is represented by Washingtonia palms, shrubby sages and a young forest of *Nolina recurvata*. A special rockery was created for the Mexican cactus garden, but this poses real problems for weeding since no chemicals are allowed. By the beach, an underwater nature trail has now evolved for guided visits only. Between and around these managed plantings extend open and wooded stretches of local *maquis*.

There was nothing theoretical about this undertaking. Clément and the Conservatoire botanists went tracking plants and photographing landscapes all over the world. It was an exhilarating adventure on a shoestring budget (sometimes their own). The same spirit of enthusiastic enterprise inspires the team that runs the Rayol today, from the director Caroline Petit to the bookshop managers Sophie and Frédéric to the head gardener Stan Alaguillaume, who organizes the Rayol's annual autumn plant fair, Gondwana. Philippe Deliau, originally Clément's assistant, now a designer with his own agency (see pp. 58–61), has since helped recreate other Conservatoire properties on the Mediterranean, such as Serre de la Madone in Menton, or Paulille, Alfred Nobel's amazing dynamite factory in the Roussillon.

A 'planetary' garden on the French Riviera has special meaning at a time when native and invasive species are a worldwide concern. Collectors, many of them British, have been acclimatizing exotics here for over two centuries. When Gilles Clément began working here, eucalyptus, acacias and callistemons were already naturalized. Clément's work has been controversial in his resistance to native plant purism and the Domaine du Rayol, which he still oversees regularly, has become an experimental centre for exotic introductions as well as for plants involved in the specifically Mediterranean dynamic of fire resistance. The gardeners keep testing and developing new varieties.

A visit to the Domaine is both enjoyable and educational. Any amount of information is readily available but once you are in the garden, nothing obstructs the flow. Some sixty thousand visitors come yearly. Most are delighted, but some are disappointed by the ecological management: no one mows grasses that go dormant in dry summer weather or meadows that have not yet gone to seed; fallen leaves are left among the trees, which are pruned only to keep views open. Gardeners at the Rayol learned early on to keep the paths raked to reassure visitors of their continuing activity. After all, the very point of the garden is to explore natural dynamics. Those who can return regularly get caught up watching – and feeling – the garden in constant evolution. As Christian Desplats, the Conservatoire's former regional representative, explains: 'We are trying to help visitors learn that a Mediterranean garden is magnificent in spring, superb in the autumn and marvellous in the winter ... but dry in summer.'[6] But even summer has its charms. Caroline Harbouri, when president of the Mediterranean Garden Society, visited early one summer morning: 'We came out on to a little opening perched above the sea and sat quietly for a while on a bench under a pine tree, looking down the steep rocks on to the clear, turquoise water of a little inlet, or *calanque* as they are called in this part of the world. Among the simple, abiding pleasures of the Mediterranean are the scents of pines and of sun-warmed beaten earth, the sight of sunlight sparkling on the sea, the sounds of insects humming, of branches stirring in a slight breath of air, of the faint mewing of seagulls somewhere in the distance.' She found the Rayol to be a beautiful but also 'comfortable' garden.[7]

Domaine du Rayol, French Riviera | Gilles Clément
The grand axis from the 1940s, reworked by Clément in 1989, begins under the pergola of the South African garden. Clément, although a leading ecologist, accepts geometry and loves long straight lines.

Domaine du Rayol, French Riviera | Gilles Clément

Head gardener Stan Alaguillaume, organizer of the autumn
plant fair, seen here in the Subtropical American garden,
the only area watered in summer (opposite left); *Syagrus
romanzoffiana* palms (opposite right); agaves, dasylirions
and yuccas stay warm thanks to a shale mulch (above);
the Hôtel de la Mer seen from the coastal path (above right);
and Australian acacias, with *A. calamifolia* in the foreground
and the blue *A. covenyi* behind (right).

MEDITERRANEAN JAPANESE

In the 1950s, a farsighted promoter acquired the peninsula of Cala Rossa in southern Corsica, piece by piece, from the daughters of local peasant families. He resold it in lots with the stipulation, surprising for the time, that no non-native plants be introduced. There was still no road, and trade was so slow that he offered prospective buyers a donkey and a second-hand *deux-chevaux* automobile to help with land clearance and access! Decades later, jet-set millionaires and celebrities assembled these properties into a gated community well protected from expanding hordes of summer tourists. In the early 1990s, landscape designer Erik Borja was asked to create an ideal Mediterranean garden in one of these domains.

Borja was born in Algeria and trained as an artist in Paris before establishing himself at his family property, Domaine des Clairmonts, in the Rhône valley. Like Fernando Caruncho and Gilles Clément, he calls himself a 'gardener' but works more as a sculptor than a horticulturalist or botanist, counting the bulldozer among his favourite design tools. His art owes much to a long romance with Japan, which began in Kyoto in 1977, an inspiration he has developed at Les Clairmonts. The landscapes of southern Corsica already seemed to Borja like a Japanese garden writ large, with their mountain ridges melting into the horizon, their natural harmonies of granite rock and scrubland cascading around the naturally layered branches of junipers and Corsican pines (*Pinus laricio*).[8]

The garden site has seafront east, south and west. Borja did not attempt to impose a Japanese style here as he had done in a neighbouring property but incorporated existing elements. Small islands just off the beach perfectly represent the traditional symbols of crane and tortoise with their upright and rounded rocks. The Corsican *maquis*, once thinned, revealed ancient junipers, tree heathers, pines and arbutus naturally shaped by wind and salt, all rising among big boulders. In this region, natural heaps of granite slabs inspire local gardeners to shore up earth with similar stacks, in the way people elsewhere make drystone constructions. Corsican custom thus already provided a feature that looked Japanese.

The whole garden displays a constant balance between volumes, textures and tones, closed and open space, transparency and mystery. Its parts are connected by serpentine paths with fine detailing in their pavings. High drama is reserved for carefully framed sea views and trees sculpted into cloud shapes by Borja's assistant and master pruner, Loïc Belviso. Many exotic varieties of plant have been added, chosen for shapes and colours that blend in seamlessly. Transitions and boundaries are always blurred.

Borja explains that he wanted to bring out 'the living energy emanating from these surges of stone which seem at once immobile and dynamic'. He insists with some pride that, as an artist, faced with such compelling beauty, he had to be self-effacing and let Nature speak. At the same time, and with equal pride, he points out that two-thirds of the present garden is of

OPPOSITE AND ABOVE Designer Erik Borja's own sand and stone Zen garden at Les Clairmonts on the mainland (opposite), and the south Corsican landscape (above) that seemed to him like a Japanese garden writ large.

his own making. Hundreds of truckloads of soil, rocks from nearby Bonifacio and dozens of mature trees were imported to create the contours of the slope and the plant tapestry as they exist today. Hidden below the surface are layers of drainage pipes, lighting cables and water ducts for the open spaces, which, although left to rough grass, are kept green in summer. The copses and groves are also watered by aspersion to reduce the salt on foliage. Careful observation of the microclimate was required to consolidate all of this, and, after more than a decade of often violent weather, there have been no landslides and only one fallen tree.

In conventional terms, this garden is 'natural' because of its irregularity of contour and roughness of texture. Perspectives are occasionally centred on a single focal point (in the Western manner), though this is always a dramatic tree or rock, never a statue. More often, asymmetry prevails (in the Japanese manner), voids counting as much as volumes. This is not, however, a naturalist's garden. There is no attempt to observe and recreate balanced, self-sustaining ecosystems dependent on partnerships with other species: Borja's sense of nature depends mainly on highly controlled scenography. Nor does he distill raw

Peninsula Garden, Corsica | Erik Borja
Truckloads of rich soil and hidden watering networks make possible a wide range of species, including local rosemary and lentisk, but also exotic azaleas, pittosporum and grevilleas.

material into symbol with a subsequent reduction of scale as the Japanese do. He works with a vast, existing landscape on its own scale, hiding human intervention as much as he can to create an illusion of natural spontaneity – not at all a Japanese aim. This behind-the-scenes staging, this veneration of artificial wilderness, recalls rather works of European picturesque and Romantic movements.

Sightlines connecting sea and land are important for any seascape. Mediterranean topography has for millennia allowed sailors and fishermen to look back not only at beacons and lighthouses but at chapels and shrines perched high above the beaches, intended also for their protection. Horden and Purcell relate that 'under the Roman thalassocracy, the coastal villas of the rich often took over the locations of seamarks and their confident display came to symbolize the quality of life in an age that had tamed the sea's perils'.[9] Today, many seafront properties aim rather at discretion: the Rayol, the properties at Antiparos or Argentario (see pp. 108–119) have been camouflaged as much as possible. The Cala Rossa property, often used for entertaining, is designed for a seafront approach, the road entrance reserved for service. Guests arrive at one of the two wharfs, to be guided up clearly defined paths to the house. Even without special events, the owner often stays on his yacht, preferring to admire his garden through binoculars from the sea. The pleasures of immersion are reserved, most of the time, for the people who work here.

Both the French Riviera and southern Corsica are cosmopolitan hotspots today for seafront tourism. The gated property with its refined scenography and the public park with its evolving ecosystems represent two different approaches to the globalization of Mediterranean coastlines.

Peninsula Garden, Corsica | Erik Borja
A two-hundred-year-old juniper pruned in the Japanese cloud manner (above). The path from the landing stage to the house (opposite) had to be wide and flat to accommodate stiletto heels.

EMPORIUM:
THE GARDENS OF VENICE

The whole Mediterranean consists of movement in space.

Fernand Braudel, 1949[1]

If the term 'vernacular' applies to rural communities ingeniously adapting local resources to meet basic needs, 'emporium' at first glance suggests just the opposite: urban centres trade goods uprooted from their places of origin and immediate function, assign exchange rather than use values, then redistribute them. And yet the ancient historian Strabo considered agriculture and trade, even piracy, to be interdependent, as had Aristotle before him.[2] Vernacular crafts have provided objects for commercial exchange, for both basic and luxury markets, since at least 5000 BC.[3] Far from linking trade with the growth of cities, the historians Horden and Purcell find that even small villages in the ancient Mediterranean were linked by market 'connectivity'.[4] The biodiversity experts agree: 'Mediterranean polyculture is more than an agronomic category, but an integral part of a network of long-distance commerce, representing energy and information exchanges.'[5] Any discussion of the Mediterranean vernacular needs to include sea-borne trade, both coastal and far-flung.

Venice was for centuries the world's most fabulous emporium. Here the very soil is mobile, created

PAGE 182 AND OPPOSITE ABOVE Venice has so often been described and depicted that every boatman seems to live in a picture postcard. But tourism, for better or worse, is the new 'connectivity'.

BELOW AND OPPOSITE BELOW The Grand Canal, with a Veronese-like marriage of sky and sea (below). The view from the San Giorgio tower of the cloister gardens and the Giudecca, where the famous Eden garden was once situated (opposite below).

by refugees out of consolidated marshlands in the eighth century. Still today, composed partly of refuse and backfill dredged from canals, it is subject to constant erosion and sedimentation. The early mud constructions were gradually reinforced with brick and stone from Ischia, but the whole city still stands on deeply planted wooden poles. On *terra firma,* vernacular builders extract local materials on site so that houses share the colours and textures of their settings. In Venice, walls rise directly from shimmering water.[6] The poet Gabriele d'Annunzio defined the 'essential spirit of Venice' as 'an inextinguishable flame seen through a veil of water'.[7] As the art historian Paul Hills puts it: 'No city built on land can offer so brilliant and so strange an intermingling...' The very place seems rootless and floating.

And yet, contrary to prevailing opinion, Venice has always contained green and growing spaces – orchards, fields, and market, monastery and pleasure gardens. Why is precious living space kept open still today? In earlier times, the need for self-sufficiency under siege was reason enough. Later Venice became a hub for spices, pharmaceuticals and rare exotics, and every family plot became medicinal. But there is more than this: experts who have perused the many sources of information recounting the city's garden history, both the international critic John Dixon Hunt and local specialist Ida Tonini,[8] suggest that gardens in Venice constitute an essential part of local identity. Perhaps the green plots scattered throughout the city's fabric offer the comforting illusion of solidity, of rootedness? 'The trauma of separation from solid earth is powerful here,' writes Tonini. Hunt quotes this lovely description published in 1902: 'You think perhaps there are no gardens in Venice... Really, if you but knew it, almost every palace hides a garden, nestling beneath its balconies, and every high wall hems in a wealth of green, studded with broken statues, quaint arbors festooned with purple grapes, and white walks bordered by ancient box; while every roof that falls beneath a window is made a hanging garden of potted plants and swinging vines.'[9] This is true still today.

MASKS

The logic of place in Venice is unique, starting with the limitations imposed on the city by the lagoon and its wetlands. Ida Tonini points out: 'Gardens in Venice are made of earth, water, stone, and especially of light, changing light reflected in water.' She adds: 'They are also invaded several times a year, sometimes for hours, by salt water.' Venice has its own forms of beauty but also of violence.

Confined space is the most obvious constraint on architecture. However wealthy, the Venetian merchant elite could not expand its palaces, only intensify and enrich their ornamentation. Builders were also subject to limits on weight and depth, leading to a strange gap between appearance and function. The well-heads present in every courtyard in fact hide underground cisterns catching rainwater from roofs. Soil depth is merely apparent. Earthworms cannot survive in Venetian soil, defeated by salt water not far down. Tall trees must be regularly cut back. Similarly, Paul Hills points out that richly ornate palace façades seen from canals give little clue to the volumes behind. Columns that look like solid marble are brick with a marble facing. The American writer Henry James praises the Venetian 'beauty of surface, of tone, of detail'.[10] Hills admires these effects in art and crafts from mosaics to glass to silks: 'Such markings, mottling, freckles and speckles, introduce organic gradation into the geometric order of colour and tone,' he notes, like so many 'organic waves'.[11] They also disguise form, depth, mass and volume. Such subtle disguises must bring to mind the Venetian tradition of masks.

Similar ambiguities concerning appearance and substance affect definitions of public and private space in house and garden. Venetian palaces, like houses in Amsterdam, were organized around trade, with storage space for goods just inside the public water door, much more important than the street gate. Gardens were private, hidden behind high walls, but the latter were often interrupted by wrought iron gates, miradors or actual windows (all now usually

BELOW AND OPPOSITE A typical courtyard 'well', which in fact hides a cistern to collect water from the surrounding roofs (below). A modern version of the traditional mirador, cut in a wall in the Bauer Palladio garden designed by architect Giuseppe Rallo (opposite).

blocked off) to suggest inner magnificence. Lattices and *claustra*, indoors and out, create patterns of light and shade in both directions, blurring shapes and half-hiding what is beyond or within. Many Venetian gardens, including those belonging to religious orders, have a *casino* or *biblioteca* in their far depths, a shallow, formal façade in brick or stone much like a stage setting and indeed sometimes designed by famous scenographers. These provide, as John Dixon Hunt says, 'an interesting means of ending a short garden vista, providing a destination for a short walk and view back to the house'.[12] But, through the centuries, they also sheltered a great range of public and private activities that intermingled in all kinds of ways: philosophical debating societies, secret political meetings and amorous encounters (including Byron's). Hunt associates them with 'scenes of anticipation and privacy or alternatively of intimacy and entrance being denied'.[13] Eighteenth-century art sometimes depicts masked figures coming out of the side doors of walled gardens. This complex organization of display and concealment was especially important for the women of Venice, celebrated for their oft-painted beauty but relatively cloistered in this city set right at the crossroads between East and West. Venetian palaces often have shallow loggias and roof terraces (*altanas*), garden spaces for catching the breeze in summer, where ladies, themselves unseen, could admire both the garden below and the bustle of urban life outside.

Nothing shows better the peculiar balance of public and private space in Venetian cityscapes than the violence done to it by Napoleon. His ambitious projects for public gardens mixed open, formal avenues (quite ill adapted to Mediterranean summers) and curving, 'English'-style parks. Venice had its own geometries. Frederick Eden, a late nineteenth-century English gardener in Venice, remarked that 'the universal measure that rules at Venice is the square, and the square is never square'[14] (appearances again at odds with reality). This applied equally to the public *campo*, the large courtyards shared by several neighbouring houses and the courtyards of private palaces. The typical

ABOVE In a beautiful private family garden designed in the 1920s, the door giving directly onto the canal has great importance from the inside but remains discreet seen from the outside.

OPPOSITE At Palazzo Soranzo Cappello, restored by Giuseppe Rallo, the seventeenth-century *casino*, or pavilion, sits at the far end of the rectangular main garden, facing the house (opposite above). Where the marble facing has fallen away, the less heavy brick construction is revealed (opposite below).

Venetian garden was for centuries a long, walled rectangle in which seeming symmetry was constant, often bilateral, like the 'opening of butterfly wings'. A pergola was obligatory, either along the central axis, set at right angles to it, or along a sidewall. The main path might be surrounded by rectangles of fruit trees, flowers or vegetables. There was nothing cold, rigid or even architectural about this formality, very different from the French style Napoleon was imposing. The Venetian version remained productive and seasonal. Eden wrote from oft repeated experience: 'In a warm climate there are few things more enjoyable than a stroll, even in August, under a vine pergola. You walk in deep shade, the fierce sun held outside, the big bunches of grapes, black and purple, yellow and golden, all the promise of a rich harvest, hanging down to knock your hat, to blob your nose, feast your eye, and tempt your lips.'[15]

The very light of Venice makes form and line sensuous and mobile. Eden, also a painter, notes that 'changes in colour are as great from day

to day, and sometimes from hour to hour, as in more northern climes from month to month, or even from season to season'.[16] But movement also comes from the use to which spaces are put. Hills points out that even the most solid monuments of Venice are designed to be enjoyed from varied and ever-changing viewpoints by people walking. A Bostonian couple who often visited the Edens claimed that, in their garden, 'one can take a walk in all seasons, have tea impeccably served, gather flowers, listen to a fashionable violinist (Frontali) on an informal evening, gather after a sad winter funeral (that of Robert Browning)'.[17] Venetian gardens were, and still are, spaces for the many everyday activities of elegant living.

The traditional gardens still surviving in Venice are often attached to hotels or institutions that remain ambiguously private and public. Kitchen plots persist mainly in monasteries. Private houses display elaborate window boxes but their inner gardens can be half-glimpsed from bridges or canals. All are inseparable from the buildings and setting; all involve 'graded views' of a special sort, where planes are layered vertically as well as horizontally. The boundaries are always buildings, water and sky. It is still true, as Eden claimed, that 'there is no other soil and climate so full of whim and fantasy'.[18]

OPPOSITE, ABOVE AND RIGHT The famous roof-terrace gardens, or *altanas* (opposite), originally intended to keep women from the public eye. Windows and outer walls (above and right) still almost always display the 'tangle of plants and flowers' so admired by Henry James.

COSMOPOLITAN VERNACULAR

The hero of Henry James's novella, *The Aspern Papers* (1888), is fascinated by 'a garden in the middle of the sea'.[19] The novelist was inspired by the Palazzo Soranzo Cappello, also lovingly described by Italian poet Gabriele d'Annunzio in *The Flame of Life* (1913). These gardens were restored in 2004 by architect Giuseppe Rallo, who has respected the site's history and maintained classic Venetian style while introducing some contemporary inspiration, both naturalistic and modernist. A long formal rectangle, divided by the classic central path, extends from the seventeenth-century palace to a *casino* with imposing columns. The door from the palace opens onto a raised stone terrace flanked by statues of Roman emperors and partly contained by a low wall.

ABOVE AND OPPOSITE The house terrace at Palazzo Soranzo Cappello, restored by Giuseppe Rallo, leads towards grass and carpets of wood hyacinth (above); a door connects the formal garden and the *brollo*, or field (opposite above); the *brollo* with one of its pergolas (opposite below).

Each section of the garden thereafter is slightly lower and less formal than the previous one. On another side of the palace is a large *brollo*, or field, once much larger and used for bullfights, horse races (d'Annunzio once raced here with actress Eleonora Duse) and even, in recent decades, for outdoor cinema. Today, in the reduced space remaining, Rallo has the rough grass cut at different heights to clarify the formal lines in a soft manner. Above all, he has brought back the pergolas, set at right angles, that d'Annunzio described: 'In the garden, the guests had dispersed along the walks and under the vine-trellises... The hidden stars of the jessamine shrubs yielded their acute perfume in the shadow; the odour of the fruits too was strong and even heavier than in the island gardens. A vivid fertilizing power emanated from that small space of cultivated earth that was enclosed like an exiled thing by its girdle of water, becoming all the more intense from its banishment...'[20]

John Dixon Hunt and Ida Tonini both agree on the continuing persistence of rustic style in Venetian gardens, still extant today even next to palaces. There are always fruit trees and pergolas mixing grapes and wisteria, and sometimes squares of vegetables as well. D'Annunzio's notebooks list, just at Soranzo Cappello, pears, peaches, almonds, plums, cherries, medlars, apricots and strawberries, along with the roses. The Eden garden, part reconverted market garden, included at its height a potager intermingling artichokes and acanthus. Eden explains, 'It is delightful to pick one's strawberries and cut one's tea rose from the same bed',[21] adding, 'We thought, and think, the mixture of the useful with the beautiful gives the latter greater value.'[22] The 'we' he mentions includes himself and his wife Caroline, née Jekyll, elder sister to the famous Gertrude,[23] who, in England, elaborated a painterly mode of gardening that surely influenced the Caetanis at Ninfa (see pp. 146–51).

Hunt wonders if his own discomfort with the 'productive' gardens of Venice may not stem from the usual preoccupation of garden historians with design highlights rather than everyday gardening – the vernacular, in fact. Questioning the very term 'productive', Hunt concludes that it 'posits a distinction between utility and pleasure or even beauty that is largely a modern one'. It is also a northern one: garden historians have yet to join the scientists and ecologically minded historians in treating the Mediterranean as a region that needs its own definitions.

What is remarkable in Venice is that vernacular gardens survive through centuries in the midst of legendary luxury and sumptuous ornamentation. One main reason may be the very importance of the city's merchant economy. For Venice the emporium was also a major supplier, not only of market produce but also of medicinal plants and botanical rarities. Locally grown and imported treasures intermingled. Tonini remarks: 'The interest and curiosity for whatever nature may produce that is rare and marvellous compelled navigators and plant hunters already in the days of Marco Polo. Through Venice came plants like rhubarb, aloes, sandalwood and cinnamon.' Hunt documents thoroughly the local growth of this commerce, including the sixteenth-century establishment of colleges of herbalists and Europe's first botanical gardens by Venetians. The Republic never despised trade as vulgar, as did land-based aristocracies; similarly, it respected productive gardening to the point of deciding, by decree, that

herbalists practised a 'nobile arte'. Venice was also a pioneer publishing centre that produced the first great treatises on gardening and agriculture, in particular *The Dream of Poliphilus*, still inspirational today.[24]

For centuries, Venice remained 'a city which made men aware of identity and difference'.[25] The presence of foreigners did not dilute the city's own distinctiveness, even during its nineteenth-century 'decadence'. Henry James saw the essence of the city in the humblest of its gardens, still a unique blend of use and beauty, public and private space – the ferryman's arbour: 'The elements are complete – the trio of air and water and of things that grow. Venice without them would be too much a matter of the tides and the stones. Even the little trellises of the *traghetti* count charmingly as reminders, amid so much artifice, of the woodland nature of man. The vine-leaves, trained on horizontal poles, make a roof of chequered shade for the gondoliers and ferrymen, who doze there according to opportunity, or chatter or hail the approaching "fare"...'[26]

ABOVE AND OPPOSITE Trade, even piracy, fed Venice for centuries, notably the looting of Constantinople in 1451. But the city was also an experimental laboratory, developing and redistributing ideas, goods, plants. Monastery gardens played an important role in this process.

MESURA

Keep watch on measure; in all things best is the when and how much...

Hesiod, *Works and Days*, c. 700 BC[1]

PAGE 196 At Ariant, the gardener's contribution, especially pruning, takes its cues from natural growth. It does not just create a look but establishes a continuing partnership.

Nineteenth-century Romantic poets reinvented Mediterranean poetry much as they transformed southern landscapes: historical evidence yielded to the projections of the artistic imagination. Much admired were the troubadours, southern French poets who had influenced Dante and Petrarch, famous for their celebration of passion outside marriage. It was easy to see them as rebel artists defending freedom, fighting law with love. A southern historian, however, lists four cardinal 'virtues' valued in twelfth-century troubadour society: *joven* (youth, enthusiasm), *joi* (joy), *largueza* (generosity) and, finally, *mesura*. The first three were easy to assimilate into the Romantic vision, but the fourth? Troubadour poetry – highly formulaic – was in fact sung. 'Mesura' suggests the harmonies of music and verse, a sense of pacing, of timing. It suggests also harmony, not only with the beloved but also with the rules of 'corteza' as imposed by the community, the famous courts of love.[2] It was in the spirit of *mesura* that the Venetian architect Carlo Scarpa (1906–78) once wrote: 'Poetry is attained through rigour, geometry, measure...'[3] Or, to borrow the words of another poet, W. H. Auden: 'Those who refuse all formal restrictions don't know what fun they're missing.'[4]

RIGHT AND OPPOSITE Ninfa's 'Romantic' ruins are often perceived as a display of human endeavour overpowered by natural energies, but this is a carefully maintained illusion. The balance between plants and masonry is constantly readjusted.

ROMANTIC CONTRADICTIONS

Romantic models from England and France held sway in much of Italy for almost two centuries, even among Italians.[5] The hero of Henry James's *Aspern Papers* spoke like a true Romantic when he said of his garden: 'Personally I liked it better as it was, with its weeds and its wild, rough tangle, its sweet, characteristic Venetian shabbiness.'[6] 'Picturesque' taste led many northerners to love the Mediterranean vernacular only at its poorest and dirtiest. 'Shabbiness' in human dwellings, like 'weeds' or 'wilderness' in nature, was a form of apparent disorder that might be taken, or mistaken, for liberty from constraint. This vision chooses to ignore any alternative order, other laws or internal necessities such as those governing rural architecture, social process or biology.

ABOVE Napoleonic imperialism in Venice helped foster the kind of Romantic vision that cherished elegiac decadence. Many northern tourists today, heirs to this sensibility, still find decay picturesque.

In landscape art, the great test is pruning. Frederick Eden, writing about his garden in Venice, expresses sympathy for both the Romantic attitude and the vernacular, indeed adopting the latter to the extent of making a good living as a farmer in the lagoon! His writing is full of revealing contradictions, which never embarrass him. As a Romantic Englishman, he professes that 'our individual taste loves vegetation as Nature grows it rather than as man clips it... As much as possible we give Nature her head...' Yet elsewhere he asserts that growth in the south is 'so fast that the scissors and knife and billhook must be kept at work to let in air and light'. Similarly, he finds the Italians so 'lazy' that 'well-swept paths, the close-cut lawns, the borders without a weed, the plants trimmed and staked, all the tidiness that goes to the keeping of an English garden, is seldom found abroad'.

Ninfa (see pp. 146-51) has been baptized 'the most Romantic garden in the world'. The discourse surrounding this enchanting place contains the same internal contradictions as Eden's. For curator Lauro Marchetti, 'Romantic' first means 'appealing to the senses and the imagination rather than the mind'. But Ninfa was also a refuge for many distinguished intellectuals, scientists and writers. Like many other Italian gardens, Ninfa kept alive the Epicurean tradition of philosophical and political exchange in green groves. Marchetti adds 'liberty' to his definition of Ninfa's Romanticism and his example concerns pruning. He remembers walking with Princess Lelia and encountering a plant spilling onto a path. He proposed to cut it back but she instructed him to redirect the path rather than inhibit the plant. Charles Quest-Ritson, Ninfa's almost official chronicler, concurs that 'one of the principles of managing the garden today is that plants should be allowed to express themselves fully and naturally'. But elsewhere he judges that 'Lelia set out to cultivate the image of a garden on the verge of collapse – of Nature just about to gain the upper hand – even though all these appearances of naturalism were a carefully constructed illusion ... controlled naturalness – artful artlessness – was central to her thinking'.

Ninfa, Lazio | Caetani family

At Ninfa, restoration of some two hundred houses and seven churches requires daily inspection. Existing mortar has been carefully analyzed. Restoration work uses only the mixture appropriate for each period.

Great care is indeed required to maintain the illusion of imminent collapse at Ninfa. The ruins are restored scrupulously to the extent that the mortar used for twelfth-century remnants is not the same mix as for later ones. Plants must be cut back often so they do not reduce walls to rubble. The fear of not pruning at the right moment, just before the walls crumble, can even give Lauro and Stella Marchetti sleepless nights! It would seem that *mesura* – pacing, timing – actually counts a great deal in Romantic Ninfa. There is of course a magic in this garden that goes beyond these quibbles about philosophy and discourse. Ninfa's impact owes a lot to the Marchettis' desire to make plants and people happy, to create what Lauro calls 'giardini dell'anima'. To this end he has newly planted a rootsprout from an olive tree growing at Gethsemane, and regards the punctuating China rose 'Mutabilis', found all over the gardens, as a symbolic union of east and west. *Mesura,* as the troubadours well knew, is not the enemy of passion but its partner.

Ninfa, Lazio | Caetani family

Ninfa's water, full of moving plants and ever-changing reflections, sometimes quiet and sometimes cascading, easily creates a Romantic mood. It remains a constant 10–12 degrees year round, and its trout are famous.

ARCADIA IN MALLORCA

An alternative paradise, a summer-dry landscape garden where pruning has long held pride of place, is Heidi Gildemeister's domain in northern Mallorca. She and her husband settled some thirty years ago on a site she describes as 'tucked between the mountains and the sea. The fields lie at an altitude of around 1,000 feet (300 metres), with both north and south exposure. Frost is rare, and yearly rainfall varies between 18 and 49 inches (45 to 125 cm).'[7] The garden today covers some four hectares, and Gildemeister has become famous worldwide for her gardening books.

The couple chose to live on long-abandoned farmland, far from the crowds: 'We found overgrazed fields, a neglected pine forest (*Pinus halepensis*) and the remains of a centuries-old oak forest (*Quercus ilex*). These ancient oaks became the backbone of our garden and its principal theme.' Along their five-kilometre access road is a watchtower that once alerted local populations to sea raiders. Nearby, Gildemeister discovered secret caves with remnants of older human occupation. She recalls: 'I had to make the best of what I found – bare stone and

Ariant, Mallorca | Heidi Gildemeister

Ariant has exposures all around the compass, centred on the house: facing north, towards the sea (below); the rugged valley northeast (opposite above); and west, nearer the house, planting beween wild olive trees (opposite below).

rock and a spring that ran dry in August. Yet I wanted to create beauty around the house. As I do always, I took advantage of the few elements that were there: the rocks, a few lentisk (*Pistacia lentiscus*), the distant horizon. I sheared the tangled mass of lentisk, so they would fill in while the few wild olive trees and ancient oak were delivered of dead wood. I was patient for them to grow. At the time, I took little interest in what was happening beyond the garden fence. We restored old buildings and I picked mushrooms, prepared chutney, made my own clothes, dried flower arrangements... Until one day, I discovered that I had to explore drought tolerance, onto which I started to focus my energy... I remember well that, most of all, I wanted to "do my own thing", let nothing influence me (no "English garden", which at the time was the fashion)... With a stonemason, we built over three winters the garden paths, a time-consuming undertaking, yet worthwhile and a first approach to landscaping which became my passion and still is.'

Gildemeister's layout was determined in the simplest possible manner: she selected the best flat spaces and connected them with curving paths, as horizontal and harmonious as possible. Since then, her efforts have gone into 'creating depth, the right volumes: my preoccupations

were the ones of a painter for the colours, of a sculptor for the volumes, of a plantswoman for the right plants, of a collector of plants, a photographer and so forth.' In those early days, her husband had resumed sheep farming and they shared enthusiastic lunchtime conversations about his experiments with animal breeds and her 'endless cuttings' for plant reproduction. The garden has evolved as concentric rings moving out from the house. Gildemeister's most recent addition is her Sheep Park, under and around ancient olive trees, where she experiments with plants that grazing animals will leave alone, such as *Euphorbia dendroides*: 'For those who can manage them, sheep grazing under olive trees add greatly to the atmosphere of a grove.' Hidden fencing protects the heart of the garden from the animals. Transitions here always flow from one scene, one plane, to another.

Gildemeister's approach has always been partnership with her site, even with dramatically bared rocks and cruelly dry summers: 'I got to know the available plants more intimately and learned about their likes and dislikes, as one does with a friend. A friendship enduring over time differs from that of a recent acquaintance, and I cherish those plants that have proved their worth over the years.' She communes with her garden, progressing through observation and improvisation: 'The plants have told me which places they like.' Self-seeders are cherished and kept whenever possible. For each scene, intimate or extensive, she 'must decide which ones can stay and eliminate the rest'. Her selection is not made just for looks but with a view to producing healthy, enduring plants.

Her main activity in the garden is pruning. She practises 'creative shaping' to establish or maintain harmony among neighbours. She prunes 'from within, branch by branch, letting this one expand, limiting another to give a neighbour a chance'. Clipping right after flowering helps plants live a long time. Now she can say: 'Every inch of my ten acres is covered with healthy growth.'

This is a garden composed mainly of groupings of shrubs and trees among boulders and rocks, the northwestern part dominated by oaks, the south by olive trunks and crowns. Gildemeister organizes everywhere a progression from near to far, from garden to woodland, hills and mountains and, in the north, the sea. Close-up detailing reveals a mosaic of mixed ground covers, tiny bulb populations and choice rare plants framed here and there by a rock, a tree trunk or a picturesque stump. There are many small tables with two chairs, facing not each other but the view. Her goal is always harmony rather than variety for its own sake: 'A natural

Ariant, Mallorca | Heidi Gildemeister
The western path, where boulders crowd close to wild olives rising from a shaped undergrowth of *Pistacia lentiscus*, *Rhamnus alaternus* and *Cneorum tricoccon* (opposite). The natural swimming pool (below).

balance makes the gardener feel at peace in a garden, rather than at war on a battlefield – pulling up and tearing down, turning over the soil, and spraying poisonous products. A natural garden also places fewer demands on the gardener, and it can be sustainable.' She advises her readers to 'know your land' and suggests they 'sit at your future doorstep, watch the sun rise or set, listen to the sounds of animals'.

This approach is a model of *mesura*, 'ecologically sound' not in respect to doctrine but because of gardening practice linked for decades to a deep understanding of the logic of place. Gildemeister advises frugal management that depends, like Hesiod's, on the 'how much' and the 'when' – watering only when needed, for example. Her sense of timing, of seasonal variation, goes deep: 'Although a Mediterranean garden can have flowers in bloom throughout the year, it does not have to be designed for constant display. Expectation is important, too, as one awaits in joyful anticipation the opening of a bud or the ripening of fruits.' She is well aware that her approach has peasant roots: 'It helps to remember that, in times past, the various elements that shaped such a garden nearly always emerged from necessity, often from the constraints that life around the Mediterranean Basin imposed on people... No wonder that food is ever present in Mediterranean life. Such limitations and restrictions challenged the imagination of the Mediterranean peoples, who responded with great ingenuity and style.'[8]

Ariant, Mallorca | Heidi Gildemeister
Exact limits between garden and setting are deliberately blurred. An agave finds a precarious hold among native euphorbias and pistachios (opposite); an aloe faces south (above).

Gildemeister's ideal resembles that of the biodiversity specialists Jacques Blondel and his team, who recommend for future landscape management an 'agro-silvo-pastoral system' that may well have been practised on the Gildemeisters' land in times past. This consists simply of land planted with food-producing trees (chestnut, olive, argan, etc.), underplanted with annual crops (cereals, vegetables, small fruit, flowers), alternating with grazing animals. They recommend this as an example of agricultural production systems that work 'in nature's image'.[9] Such iconic, balanced, Mediterranean landscapes have drawn the admiration of travellers through the centuries, for example English writer Tobias Smollett, in 1764, near the French city of Grasse: 'When I stand upon the rampart, and look round me, I can scarce help thinking myself inchanted. The small extent of country which I see, is all cultivated like a garden. Indeed, the plain presents nothing but gardens, full of green trees, loaded with oranges, lemons, citrons, and bergamots, which make a delightful appearance. If you examine them more nearly, you will find plantations of green pease

Ariant, Mallorca | Heidi Gildemeister

Ancient specimens of two tree species embrace this garden: in exposed parts, the holm oak (*Quercus ilex*, above); in protected areas, the olive (*Olea europaea*, opposite). *Euphorbia dendroides* (right), a species spared by sheep.

ready to gather; all sorts of sallading, and pot-herbs, in perfection; and plats of roses, carnations, ranunculas, anemonies, and daffodils, blowing in full glory, with such beauty, vigour, and perfume, as no flower in England ever exhibited.'[10]

For the ecologists as for the historians, however, beauty is not enough. But then neither is it for many artists. Those working on public projects such as the art trail linking Provence and Piedmont (VIAPAC, *Via per l'arte contemporanea*; see also p. 24), must meet the following criteria laid down by the sponsors. They must be used to working outdoors and mixing very different scales; integrate a social dimension, in harmony with the local population; respect local heritage and the environment; use a vocabulary and materials suitable for the austerity of the sites; take in the historic and sometimes even mystic dimensions of past site history; and use materials adapted to aggressive mountain climates for works that will have no supervision and little upkeep.[11] These rules are not so much restrictions as the conditions of harmony, of *mesura*. The first to begin work on the VIAPAC project was American artist Richard Nonas. He wrote about the abandoned village of Vière, where he established his first stone lines, that it 'continues as searing local memory and ecological longing literally marked on a human place'. The site has power because 'it has prevailed long enough to thrill us ... and because what will happen next is solely and simply up to us to decide'.[12]

The British historians Horden and Purcell remind us that 'in the Mediterranean, an unpredictable environment has been the setting – over and over again – for the improvement of human food-systems and of ecological harmony, and for the deterioration of both as a consequence of accident, aggression and greed'. They warn that 'the one great "constant" of the Mediterranean economy has been shifting along a spectrum of possibilities, not standing still ...

Ariant, Mallorca | Heidi Gildemeister

Hundreds of species flower year round, these in March (clockwise from left): *Anemone coronaria*, *Chasmanthe floribunda*, gladiolus and aloe.

Ariant, Mallorca | Heidi Gildemeister

Gildemeister has been keeping meteorological data since 1972. Knowledge of soil and growing conditions, she insists, conserves precious energy. Site character, local traditions and skills, changing weather, the experience of ages and of the passing moment challenge Mediterranean landscape art today. Is there energy? Is there time?

this history always reveals flux: there is no "balanced arcadia", no ecological state of grace...' It is precisely 'modernity' which allows us to afford tradition today, and 'not in any self-conscious spirit of tourist-pleasing folklorism'.[13]

There are indeed urgent choices to be made, to do with growth rather than decay, with community rather than isolation. The vernacular muse is being revived as an act of choice rather than nostalgia. Romantic vision still remains deeply solipsistic, preferring the piquancy of strangeness and sensation to dialogue. Many artists are exploring instead an 'interactive and embedded' connection between human identity and the land, dream and diversity, *mesura* and passion. Many are moved by vernacular Mediterranean landscapes, which, at their best, suggest a model for sustainable partnership that is very old and very new, and always full of wonder.

NOTES

Full bibliographic information for short-form citations is given in the Bibliography.

INTRODUCTION

1. Highet, p. 73.
2. As, for example, at the Grottes Chauvet in the Ardèche, France, where cave paintings closely associated with site contours date from thirty thousand years ago.
3. Penone, p. 284.
4. Blondel et al, p. 286, and preface by Peter Raven, p. xiv.
5. Blondel et al, p. 202.
6. Horden and Purcell, p. 403.
7. Blondel et al, p. 21.
8. 'In Praise of Limestone', first published in *Horizon* in July 1948, included in Auden's *Collected Shorter Poems, 1922–1957*, p. 238. Quoted and developed by Horden and Purcell, p. 5.
9. Blondel et al, 1.4 and 13.1.
10. Rackham, 'The Physical Setting', in *The Mediterranean in History*, ed. David Abulafia.
11. Blondel et al, p. 235.
12. Horden and Purcell. pp. 337 and 295ff.
13. Papanek, p. 114.
14. Papanek, p. 118.
15. Horden and Purcell, p. 272.
16. For example in Gilles Clément and Gilles A. Tiberghien, *Dans la Vallée*.
17. The same prejudices hold where scientific observation is concerned. The environmentalist Richard Mabey protests against 'the conventional wisdom that country people were too busy or too stupid to have anything other than a doggedly practical interest in wild plants'. *Weeds*, p. 108.
18. Jean Giono, *La Pierre et Arcadie... Arcadie...*, p. 84.
19. *Dans la Vallée*, p. 69. See also his *Nature, Art, Paysage* and *La Nature dans l'Art*.
20. This quotation from the philosophers Isabelle Stengers and Ilya Prigogine serves as epigraph for Chapter IV of Tiberghien's book with ecologist Gilles Clément, *Dans la Vallée*.
21. See *Nature, Art, Paysage* and *La Nature dans l'Art*. Also Udo Weilacher, *Between Landscape Architecture and Land Art*.
22. Hunt, foreword to Weilacher, p. 6.
23. Weilacher, p. 17.
24. *Dans la Vallée*, p. 161. Gilles Tiberghien, in the preface to his book on photography, *La Nature dans l'Art*, claims that moderns share with Aristotle 'a very attentive observation of natural phenomena and an interest in their

development in all of their phases', but the examples he presents are so abstract that most could be sited almost anywhere.
25. *Dans la Vallée*, pp. 184–85.
26. Michael Lancaster, p. 4.
27. *Dans la Vallée*, p. 169. Tiberghien has been fascinated with the theme of the cabin in the woods (*la cabane*) for years but always in terms of romantic isolation, whereas many of his criteria for its success fit vernacular architecture just as well. For Clément's appreciation of peasant life, see his preface to the 2003 edition of Adrienne Cazeilles, *Quand on avait tant de racines*.
28. 'Troubadour', in *Spirit of Place*, p. 278.
29. Hunt edited a colloquium in 1990 on this theme, papers published as *The Vernacular Garden*. The comments on Venice are in John Dixon Hunt, *The Venetian City Garden: Place, Typology and Perception*.
30. Horden and Purcell, p. 339.
31. Foreword to Weilacher, p. 6.

CHAPTER 1 **MOUNTAINS**

1. See Note 8.
2. Braudel, Vol. 1, 1966, pp. 26–27.
3. Giono, *Arcadie... Arcadie...*, p. 78.
4. Original project statement, 'The Art Refuges, declaration of intention by the artist', dated June 1999, first published on the website of the commissioning body, the Bureau des Compétences; see Andy Goldsworthy, *Refuges d'Art: Andy Goldsworthy*, 2010, and Louisa Jones, *New Gardens in Provence*, 2006. Quotations here are also from a personal interview conducted in Digne, September 2010.
5. A phrase invented by the artist; see the hermann de vries [sic] exhibition catalogue, *ReConnaître: les choses mêmes, herman de vries, extrait du journal de Digne*.
6. Richard Nonas, *Vière and the Middle Mountains*: www.resgeol04.org/ROUTEART.html.
7. Goldsworthy recalls his first storm in Provence: 'Just incredible to see. I have never experienced that. I think what is most unnerving is not the rising water so much as the quality of it – it is thick and dark – it is unlike water, it is something else, it is like liquid stone, earth. There is no depth to it. When water rises in Scotland it is dark and dirty, but you know there is depth to it. Here you cannot penetrate it with your eye. This is an extraordinary place.' Project statement, 1999.
8. *Refuges d'Art*, p. 160.
9. De vries catalogue, p. 18.
10. Antony Gormley, 'Cent corps de fer', *Le Courrier international*, No. 1036, 9–15 September 2010, pp. 52–55, reprinted from *The Guardian*. It is

interesting how nudity in mountain sites has become part of the neo-romantic ecology, even part of a new sports tourism. See *Le Courrier international*, No. 997, 10–16 December 2009.
11. Gilles Clément, *Le Belvédère des lichens*. See also www.surlesentierdeslauzes.fr.
12. See also in Catalonia, the Centro de Arte y Naturaleza, www.cdan.es.

CHAPTER 2 **STONEWORKS**

1. Giono, *La Pierre*, p. 12. Text written in February 1955.
2. Blondel et al, 1.2.5, 'Soils'.
3. Mary Keen, 'The Landscape at Kanonas and Strongilo', unpublished document.
4. Mary Keen, 'The Practicalities of Making a Garden', 8 November 2010, on http://thinkingardens.co.uk. In the first part of this two-part series (11 October 2010), Keen writes: 'Good gardens are places where human time stands still and you start to feel that there is something going on under the surface.'
5. Blondel et al, 10.4.4, 'Terraces', p. 229: 'Until the early 20th century, terrace cultivation remained a hallmark speciality of Mediterranean landscapes, from the mountains right down to the coast.'
6. Ambroise et al, p. 15.
7. Martineau, p. 65.
8. Graves, pp. 21–22.
9. John Dixon Hunt, *Nature Over Again: The Garden Art of Ian Hamilton Finlay*. See also Ian Hamilton Finlay, *Fleur de l'Air: A Garden in Provence*, and Ian Hamilton Finlay, *Sentences*, 2005.
10. Hunt, *Nature*, p. 141.
11. Quoted in Hunt, *Nature*, p. 128. Finlay wrote: 'Every summer, in Europe's "sculpture parks", Art may be seen savaging Nature, for the entertainment of tourists.' He argues elsewhere that 'so called sculptural ornaments should draw attention not to themselves but to the indigenous features of the woodland'.
12. Hunt, *Nature*, p. 37.
13. Both of these statements are part of his *Sentences*.
14. Hunt, p. 147.
15. Louisa Jones, *Nicole de Vésian – Gardens – Modern Design in Provence*, p. 129.
16. Her brothers' laundry, actually. There is the intriguing hypothesis put forth by Samuel Butler that Homer was really Nausicaa.
17. Disconnected sentences, quoted in Hunt, p. 39.
18. Finney, quoted in Louisa Jones, *Nicole de Vésian – Gardens – Modern Design in Provence*, p. 133.
19. Quoted in Hunt, *Nature*, p. 149.

CHAPTER 3 **EARTHWORKS**

1. Quoted on the website www.artpointfrance.org/Diffusion/penone.htm.
2. Cazeilles, pp. 130–31.
3. Blondel et al, 1.2.5, 'Soils'.
4. See Jacques Chibois and Louisa Jones, *Provence Harvest* (Stewart, Tabori & Chang, 2005), in which the great chef recalls his peasant parents selling their own potatoes and buying the neighbours', grown mere metres away, because they had better flavour.
5. Blondel et al, p. 16: 'with nowhere less than 2,300 hours of sunshine per year and more than 3,000 hours in most of the eastern and southern parts of the basin'.
6. Jean Giono, 'Il est vain de vouloir réunir...', 26 April 1961, republished in *Provence*, Gallimard, 1993.
7. Petrie Harbouri, *Our Lady of the Serpents*, Bloomsbury, 1999, p. 19.
8. Romilly, p. 40.
9. Museums in Saint-Quentin and Clermont-Ferrand, France.
10. Quoted in Tim Richardson, *Futurescapes*, p. 204.
11. See Louisa Jones, 'Moroccan Life', *Garden Design Journal*; Richardson, *Futurescapes*; and www.maurieres.ossart.com.

CHAPTER 4 **WOODWORKS**

1. Columella, *On Agriculture*, p. 9.
2. For illuminating works of ethnobotany, see Pierre Lieutaghi and Francis Hallé.
3. Blondel et al, 10.3.1, p. 217.
4. Horden and Purcell, p. 334.
5. Blondel et al, 6.1, p. 119.
6. Blondel et al, 6.1, p. 118.
7. Horden and Purcell, pp. 182 ff.
8. Tamisier, p. 20.
9. Quoted in Helen Leach, Chapter Four, 'The Taming of the "Wilderness"', pp. 100 ff.
10. A phrase used by Horden and Purcell, pp. 411 ff.
11. Homer, *The Odyssey*, p. 69.
12. Horden and Purcell, p. 459.
13. Stendhal, p. 183, entry dated 19 May 1838, Le Luc.
14. Huxley, p. 295.
15. A summary of the richly detailed and much longer research done by Helen Leach.
16. Richardson, *The Arcadian Friends*, p. 96.
17. Hunt, *Nature Over Again*, p. 129.
18. One of his *Sentences*. In the book on Fleur de l'Air, Harry Gilonis traces Finlay's quotations but was apparently unable to find a source for this one, which Finlay perhaps invented for this site.
19. Hunt, p. 168.
20. Giono, *La Pierre*, p. 86.
21. Huxley, p. 293.

22. Columella, p. 27.
23. Unpublished poem by Marc Nucera, composed in homage to a tree. See Louisa Jones, *New Gardens in Provence*.
24. See Louisa Jones, *New Gardens in Provence*, for an early presentation of La Verrière.
25. Weilacher, p. 17.
26. *Giuseppe Penone*, Académie de France à Rome Villa Medici, ed. Daniela Lancioni (Editions Hazan, 2008).

CHAPTER 5 **CLIPPED GREENERY**

1. Wharton, pp. 5–6.
2. Pearson, p. 27.
3. Harbouri, *The Mediterranean Garden*, No. 58, October 2009, p. 3.
4. Blondel et al, see 1.4.1 and 3.7.1 ff.
5. Mirabel Osler, pp. 145–52.
6. See Louisa Jones, *Nicole de Vésian – Gardens – Modern Design in Provence*.
7. Ibid.
8. Personal interviews, 2009.
9. Pearson, p. 56.
10. Nor yet the 'natural' garden Russell Page found on the roof of Le Corbusier's office building in Paris. Visiting him there in 1949, Page found the setting 'over-severe and logical' but, up top, the architect had been 'content to spread earth and, as he said, leave the birds and the wind to do the rest. So here were tufts of grass and weeds, dandelions and willow-herb and even young laburnum trees – a wild and haphazard growth from seeds blown there by the wind or left for birds.' *Education of a Gardener*, p. 266. Le Corbusier's Villa Mandrot in Le Pradet, inspired by the Mediterranean vernacular, is not on stilts but sits firmly on its hillside ... among shade trees.
11. *Modern Architecture and the Mediterranean: Vernacular Dialogues and Contested Identities*, ed. Jean-François Lejeune and Michelangelo Sabatino.

CHAPTER 6
MATORRAL, MAQUIS AND MEADOW

1. Personal communication.
2. Blondel et al, 3.1, 'Flora'. The authors again compare 'this regional richness to the mere 6,000 species of higher plants found in Europe north of the Mediterranean Basin, an area that is about three to four times greater in size!'
3. Blondel et al, 6.2. Comparable terms used in other Mediterranean-climate regions, where similar vegetation types are common, include: 'chaparral' and 'coastal sage' in California; 'matorral' and 'jaral' in Chile; 'fynbos', 'renosterveld', 'karroid shrubland'

and 'strandveld' in South Africa; and 'kwongan' and 'mallee' in southern Australia.
4. Virgil, p. 203. See also www.theoi.com/Text/VirgilGeorgics1.html#1.
5. Horden and Purcell, and David Jones.
6. Two houses designed by Deca Architecture received awards. A new phase will now involve architects such as Atelier Bow-Wow, Harry Gugger, Andreas Angelidakis, Katerina Tsigarida, Camilo Rebelo and Fuhriman Haehler, still with a view to establishing a contemporary approach to the Cycladic architecture.
7. *The Architectural Review*, December 2010, issue 1366, pp. 97–99. Text available on www.doxiadisplus.com under 'news'.
8. Hesiod, No. 2, 'Hymn to Demeter with the Myth of the Seasons'.
9. Blondel et al, 6.4, 'Old Fields'.
10. Fortescue, p. 52.
11. Doxiadis, pp. 22–23.
12. Columella, pp. 21 and 255. See also Tyrwhitt, p. 108: 'April is the busiest gardening month of the Greek year. There are more flowers in full bloom, just coming out and just going over, than at any other time.'

CHAPTER 7 **FIELD GEOMETRIES**

1. Durrell, p. 367.
2. Pliny the Younger, Letter XXIII.
3. Richardson, *The Arcadian Friends*, p. 128.
4. Cf Blondel et al, 10.5.1, 'Sylva-saltus-ager'.
5. Pitte, p. 59.
6. Blondel et al, 10.5.1, 'Sylva-saltus-ager', p. 230.
7. Jean Giono in *Arcadie... Arcadie...* has a fine description of the difference between efficient highways and what might be called 'vernacular' country roads. Avignon-based landscape architect Sébastien Giorgis, whose agency helped trace a major rail axis across Provence, recalls that, for decades, modern engineers completely disregarded 'morphology or any cultural identities embodied in the countryside to be traversed. Our work takes these factors into consideration, respects site memory and is in harmony with geographical realities. At the same time, a bullet train is not a horsecart. It cannot be disguised as such. We try to avoid uniformity and maintain harmony and spirit of place, not out of nostalgia but in a logic where economics and aesthetics can meet.' Giorgis and his colleagues practise an enlightened version of public Mediterranean landscape art.
8. Jacques Simon is a marked exception. In 1994, he proposed that living countryside could best be experienced either by 'putting on peasant boots' and exploring, day by day, year by year, or by substituting for time and space the aerial view: 'Flying over the land in a way

that allows you to interpret its structures, read it like a palimpsest, understand its layers of time, and how it came to be as it is.' He hoped that landscape art in remote rural areas would awaken public awareness and encourage producers to concentrate on quality products; that the pride of production might become in itself a kind of outdoor art, 'one of the cogs of rural renewal', creating 'the taste to learn how a region came to be and what is grown there'. Simon hoped to see 'the habit of substituting a field for a drawing board. The need for personal fulfilment but not as a gratuitous gesture, and also with ecological awareness. Indeed, to promote a new vernacular where everyone can become a creator...'

9. See Gilles A. Tiberghien, *La Nature dans L'Art*, Section 11, 'Agricultures', and John Berger, p. 23.
10. Rousseau, p. 393.
11. See Anne de Verteuil, 'Fernando Caruncho', *Garden Design Journal*, p. 16. See also Guy Cooper and Gordon Taylor.
12. All quotations from personal interviews and above references.
13. Quoted in Sitwell, pp. 5–6.
14. Quoted by Didier Simin in his preface to Giuseppe Penone, *Respirer l'Ombre*, p. 11.
15. Jean-Jacques Antier, cited in Howarth, p. 19.
16. Gosling, p. 97.
17. Elizabeth Kolbert, 'Turf War', *The New Yorker*.
18. Horden and Purcell, pp. 266 and 303.

CHAPTER 8 **GARDEN**

1. Olivier de Serres, p. 733.
2. Aude Gros de Beler and Bruno Marmiroli, p. 11. Fertility was inevitably linked to power in the founding myths. Demeter and the Assyrian goddess Innana both took revenge for rape by rendering the entire world sterile.
3. Horden and Purcell, p. 224.
4. Blondel et al, p. 353.
5. Braudel, Vol. 1, pp. 56 ff.
6. Quest-Ritson, *The English Garden Abroad* and *Ninfa: The Most Romantic Garden in the World.* See also Lauro Marchetti and Esme Howard, *Ninfa: A Roman Enchantment.*
7. Atlee, *Italian Gardens: A Cultural History.*
8. Blondel et al, p. 296.
9. Quest-Ritson, *Ninfa*, p. 223.
10. Page, p. 94.
11. Scott, p. 87.
12. Howard, p. 15.

13. Page, p. 47.
14. Pejrone, personal interview, September 2010.

CHAPTER 9 **SEASCAPES**

1. Giono, *La Pierre*, p. 122.
2. Blondel et al, 1.2, pp. 1 ff, 'The Physical Background'.
3. Blondel et al, 1.2.2., p. 10, 'Islands and Archipelagos'.
4. Quoted by Horden and Purcell, p. 134.
5. Blondel et al, p. 264.
6. Personal interview. Other sources of information about the Rayol garden include Clément, *Les Jardins du Rayol*; Lesot, *Le Domaine du Rayol*; and Louisa Jones, *French Country Garden.*
7. Caroline Harbouri, 'Domaine du Rayol', pp. 16, 17.
8. Borja, pp. 100–12.
9. Horden and Purcell, p. 125.

CHAPTER 10
EMPORIUM: THE GARDENS OF VENICE

1. The historian Fernand Braudel, quoted in Horden and Purcell, p. 144.
2. Horden and Purcell, p. 156.
3. A recent discovery in Syria confirms that some revision of the conventional views is necessary: in digs at Tell Zeidan, where 'a stone seal depicting a deer, presumably used to stamp a mark on goods', made of non-local stone and similar to one found 185 miles away, has been interpreted by archaeologists as evidence of 'specialized craft production dependent on trade and capable of acquiring luxury goods', at a time (some 5,000 years BC) before the invention of the wheel or the use of donkeys for transport. It is not so much trade that is remarkable, they claim, as the existence already of a standardized trademark. Article by John Noble Wilford.
4. Horden and Purcell, Chapter IV, p. 72.
5. Blondel et al, p. 205.
6. The constraints of the lagoon are elaborated by art historian Paul Hills, p. 9.
7. D'Annunzio, p. 48.
8. Hunt, *The Venetian City Garden*, and Tonini, 'Giardini di Venezia'.
9. Hunt, *The Venetian City Garden*, p. 10.
10. Quoted by Hills, p. 40.
11. Hills, p. 38.
12. Hunt, *The Venetian City Garden*, p. 128.
13. Hunt, *The Venetian City Garden*, p. 120. Among the many words this scholar collects, referring to

places where greenery was protected in Venice, is the word *broglio*, which evolved into the word for 'intrigue'.
14. Eden, p. 24. John Dixon Hunt points out that his true name was Hyden (Hunt, pp. 93 and 169 ff.).
15. Eden, p. 29. Eden advised pretty young women visitors to pick with their lips (p. 45).
16. Eden, p. 10.
17. Tonini, 'The Jekyll Sisters', p. 15.
18. Eden, p. 42.
19. Henry James, *The Aspern Papers*, p. 29.
20. Quoted in Tonini, 'Giardini di Venezia', p. 53.
21. Eden, p. 64.
22. Eden, p. 54.
23. Tonini, 'The Jekyll Sisters'.
24. A history well documented in Hunt's pages.
25. Hills, p. 19.
26. James, *Italian Hours*, p. 55. First published 1909.

CHAPTER 11 **MESURA**

1. Stephanie Nelson, p. 167.
2. Bec, pp. 20–21.
3. Quoted by Ida Tonini, 'Giardini di Venezia', p. 57.
4. Quoted in Amanda Cross, *Poetic Justice*, Virago, 1994, p. 197. John Dixon Hunt concludes: 'Venetian gardens prospered best when they observed forms and structures consistent with their local circumstances ... the "English" or "picturesque" garden travels abroad and endures foreign parts as awkwardly and impatiently as some of its own citizens' (*The Venetian City Garden*, p. 172).
5. Still today, until very recently, this influence partly accounts for a dearth of contemporary, locally rooted landscape art. See Helena Atlee, who also recounts the efforts of a whole generation of British gardeners in Tuscany, around 1900, to attempt a return to Renaissance classicism. See also Geoffrey Scott's rejection of romanticism in his influential book *The Architecture of Humanism*, first published 1909.
6. James, *The Aspern Papers*, p. 39.
7. Quotations are from Gildemeister's first book and personal emails.
8. Gildemeister, *Mediterranean Gardening*, p. 62.
9. Blondel et al, 13.3. 'Steps Towards Sustainability', pp. 299 ff.
10. Smollett, p. 117.
11. www.resgeol04.org/ROUTEART.html.
12. Ibid.
13. Horden and Purcell, pp. 303 and 473–75.

BIBLIOGRAPHY

Abulafia, David, ed., *The Mediterranean in History*, Thames & Hudson, 2003.

Ambroise, Régis, Pierre Frapa, and Sébastien Giorgis, *Paysages de terrasses*, Edisud, 1989.

Atlee, Helena, *Italian Gardens: A Cultural History*, Frances Lincoln, 2006.

Auden, W. H., *Collected Shorter Poems, 1922–1957*, Vintage, 1966, pp. 238–40.

Bec, Pierre, ed., *Nouvelle Anthologie de la lyrique occitane du Moyen Age: Textes avec traductions*, Aubanel, 1972.

Berger, John, *Pig Earth*, Pantheon Books, 1979.

Blondel, Jacques, James Aronson, Jean-Yves Bodiou, and Gilles Bœuf, *The Mediterranean Region: Biological Diversity in Space and Time*, Oxford University Press, 2010.

Borja, Erik, *Esprit du zen dans nos jardins*, Chêne, 2005.

Braudel, Fernand, *The Mediterranean and the Mediterranean World in the Age of Philip II*, Vols 1 and 2, Harper Colophon, 1966, first published 1949.

Cazeilles, Adrienne, *Quand on avait tant de racines*, Trabucaire, 2003.

Clément, Gilles, *Le Belvédère des lichens*, Jean-Pierre Huguet and the Parc Naturel Régional des Monts d'Ardèche, 2009.

——, *Les Jardins du Rayol*, Actes Sud, 2005.

——, and Gilles A. Tiberghien, *Dans la Vallée: Biodiversité, art et paysage*, Bayard, 2009.

Columella, *On Agriculture, Book X: The Layout of the Garden*, trans. E. S. Forster and Edward H. Heffner, Loeb Classical Library Harvard University Press, 2001.

Cooper, Guy, and Gordon Taylor, *Mirrors of Paradise: The Gardens of Fernando Caruncho*, Monacelli Press, 2000.

Craige, Sheppard, *Il Bosco della Ragnaia*, Edizioni della Ragnaia, 2004.

——, *Words in the Woods*, Edizioni della Ragnaia, 2007.

d'Annunzio, Gabriele, *The Flame of Life*, trans. Kassandra Vivaria, Colonial Press; first published by Page Editions, 1900.

Doxiadis, Cali, 'Grasses, native or otherwise', in *The Mediterranean Garden*, October 2009, No. 58, pp. 22–23.

Durrell, Lawrence, *Spirit of Place: Letters and Essays on Travel*, ed. Alan G. Thomas, Leete's Island Books, 1969.

Eden, Frederick, *A Garden in Venice*, Frances Lincoln, 2003; first published by Country Life, 1903; postface by Marie-Thérèse Weal.

Filippi, Olivier, *The Dry Gardening Handbook: Plants and Practices for a Changing Climate*, Thames & Hudson, 2008.

Finlay, Ian Hamilton, *Fleur de l'Air: A Garden in Provence*, ed. Pia Maria Simig, photographs by Volkmar Herre, introduction by John Dixon Hunt, commentaries by Harry Gilonis, Wild Hawthorn Press, 2004.

——, *Sentences*, Wild Hawthorn Press, 2005.

Fortescue, Winifred, *Perfume from Provence*, Blackwood and Sons, 1950.

Gay, Jennifer, *Greece: Garden of the Gods*, Athens News, 2004.

Gildemeister, Heidi, *Gardening the Mediterranean Way: Practical Solutions for Summer-Dry Climates*, Thames & Hudson, 2004.

——, *Mediterranean Gardening: A Waterwise Approach*, Editorial Moll, 1998.

Giono, Jean, 'Il est vain de vouloir réunir...', 26 April 1961, republished in *Provence*, Gallimard, 1993.

——, *La Pierre* and *Arcadie... Arcadie...*, Gallimard Folio, 1973.

Giuseppe Penone, exhibition catalogue, Académie de France à Rome, Hazan, 2008.

Goldsworthy, Andy, *Refuges d'Art: Andy Goldsworthy*, Gassendi Museum, Digne, 2010.

——, *Varia: Refuges d'Art*, Editions Artha, Gassendi Museum, Digne, 2004.

Gormley, Antony, 'Cent corps de fer', *Le Courrier international*, No. 1036, 9–15 Sept 2010, pp. 52–55, reprinted from *The Guardian*.

Gosling, Frances, *The Lure of the Riviera*, Robert M. McBride and Co., 1927.

Graves, William, *Wild Olives: Life in Majorca with Robert Graves*, Pimlico, 2001.

Gros de Beler, Aude, and Bruno Marmiroli, *Jardins et paysages de l'antiquité*, Vols I and II, Actes Sud, 2008.

Grove, A. T., and Oliver Rackham, *The Nature of Mediterranean Europe: An Ecological History*, Yale University Press, 2003.

Hallé, Francis, *Plaidoyer pour l'arbre*, Actes Sud, 2006.

——, and Pierre Lieutaghi, eds, *Aux origines des plantes*, Fayard, 2008.

Harbouri, Caroline, 'Dogmas', in *The Mediterranean Garden*, No. 58, October 2009, pp. 1–3.

——, 'Domaine du Rayol', in *The Mediterranean Garden*, No. 62, December 2010, pp. 12–17.

Harbouri, Petrie, *Our Lady of the Serpents*, Bloomsbury, 1999.

Harris, W. V., ed., *Rethinking the Mediterranean*, Oxford University Press, 2005.

Hesiod, *The Homeric Hymns*, and *Homerica*, ed. and trans. Hugh G. Evelyn-White, Loeb Classical Library, 1914: see also http://omacl.org/Hesiod/hymns.html.

Highet, Gilbert, *Poets in a Landscape*, Alfred Knopf, 1957.

Hills, Paul, *Venetian Colour: Marble, Mosaic, Painting and Glass, 1250–1550*, Yale University Press, 1999.

Homer, *The Odyssey*, trans. Samuel Butler, Barnes & Noble, 1993.

Horden, Peregrine, and Nicholas Purcell, *The Corrupting Sea: A Study of Mediterranean History*, Blackwell, 2000.

Howard, Esme, 'Beauty in Ruins: Ninfa', in *Historic Gardens Review*, Issue 22, December 2009, pp. 10–15.

Howarth, Patrick, *When the Riviera was Ours*, Century, 1977.

Hunt, John Dixon, *Nature Over Again: The Garden Art of Ian Hamilton Finlay*, Reaktion Books, 2009.

——, *The Venetian City Garden: Place, Typology and Perception*, Birkhäuser, 2009.

——, and Joachim Wolschke-Bulmahn, eds, *The Vernacular Garden*, Dumbarton Oaks Colloquium on the History of Landscape Architecture XIV, 1993.

Huxley, Aldous, *The Olive Tree and Other Essays*, Chatto & Windus, 1947.

James, Henry, *The Aspern Papers and Other Stories*, Könemann, 1998.

——, *Italian Hours*, First World Library, 2007; see www.1stworldlibrary.com.

Jones, David, unpublished manuscript: *Frontiers*, Chapter VII, 'Non-Maritime and Maritime Cultures: The Rise of Ancient Egypt and the Aegean Cycladic Frontier'.

Jones, Louisa, *The French Country Garden*, Thames & Hudson, 2000.

——, *Manifeste pour le jardin méditerranéen*, Actes Sud, 2012.

——, 'Moroccan Life' in *Garden Design Journal*, August 2010, No. 97, pp. 14–18.

——, *New Gardens in Provence*, Stewart, Tabori & Chang, 2006.

——, *Nicole de Vésian – Gardens – Modern Design in Provence*, Actes Sud, 2011.

——, and Gilles Clément, *Gilles Clément: Une écologie humaniste*, Aubanel, 2006.

Keen, Mary, unpublished document: 'The Landscape at Kanonas and Strongilo', November 2007.

Kolbert, Elizabeth, 'Turf War', in *The New Yorker*, 21 July 2008.

Lancaster, Michael, *The New European Landscape*, Butterworth Architecture, 1994.

Leach, Helen, *Cultivating Myths: Fiction, Fact and Fashion in Garden History*, Godwit, 2000.

Lejeune, Jean-François, and Michelangelo Sabatino, *Modern Architecture and the Mediterranean: Vernacular Dialogues and Contested Identities*, Routledge, 2010.

Lesot, Sonia, *Le Domaine du Rayol: Le jardin des Méditerranées*, Editions Gaud, 2008.

Lieutaghi, Pierre, *Petite Ethnobotanique méditerranéenne*, Actes Sud, 2006.

Marchetti, Lauro, and Esme Howard, *Ninfa: A Roman Enchantment*, Thames & Hudson, 1999.

Martineau, Alice, *Gardening in Sunny Lands*, D. Appleton and Company, 1924.

Nelson, Stephanie, *God and the Land: The Metaphysics of Farming in Hesiod and Vergil*, with a translation of Hesiod's *Works and Days* by David Grene, p. 167.

Nonas, Richard, *Vière and the Middle Mountains*, Gassendi Museum, Digne, 2010: see www.musee-gassendi.org.

Nucera, Marc, *A L'Ecoute des arbres*, Actes Sud, 2009.

Osler, Mirabel, *Secret Gardens of France*, Pavilion, 1993.

Page, Russell, *Education of a Gardener*, Harvill Press, 1995.

Papanek, Victor, *The Green Imperative: Ecology and Ethics in Design and Architecture*, Thames & Hudson, 1995.

Pearson, Dan, *Garden Inspiration*, Fuel, 2009.

Pejrone, Paolo, *Cronache da un giardino*, Mondadori Arte, 2010.

——, *I miei giardini*, Mondadori Arte, 2008.

Penone, Giuseppe, *Respirer l'Ombre*, Edition des Beaux-arts de Paris, 2008; preface by Didier Semin.

Pitte, Jean-Robert, *Histoire du paysage français*, Vol. I, Tallandier, 1986.

Pliny the Younger, *Letters*, trans. William Melmoth, revised by F. C. T. Bosanquet, Harvard Classics; P. F. Collier & Son, 1909.

Quest-Ritson, Charles, *The English Garden Abroad*, Viking, 1992.

——, *Ninfa: The Most Romantic Garden in the World*, Frances Lincoln, 2009.

Rackham, Oliver, 'The Physical Setting', in *The Mediterranean in History*, ed. David Abulafia, Thames & Hudson, 2003.

Richardson, Tim, *The Arcadian Friends: Inventing the English Landscape Garden*, Bantam Press, 2007.

——, *Futurescapes*, Thames & Hudson, 2011.

Romilly, Jacqueline de, *Sur les chemins de Sainte-Victoire*, Julliard, 1987.

Rousseau, Jean-Jacques, *Julie, or the New Heloise*, trans. and annotated by Philip Stewart and Jean Vaché, Dartmouth College, 1997.

Scott, Geoffrey, *The Architecture of Humanism: A Study in the History of Taste*, W. W. Norton, 1999.

Serres, Olivier de, *Le Théâtre d'agriculture et mesnage des champs*, Actes Sud Collection 'Thesaurus', 1996.

Simig, Pia, ed., *Solitude and Renunciation: Ian Hamilton Finlay, Two Gardens*, Kehrer, 2010; essay by Prudence Carlson.

Sitwell, Sir George, *On the Making of Gardens*, David R. Godine, 2003.

Smollett, Tobias, *Travels Through France and Italy*, Oxford World's Classics, 1979.

Stendhal (Henri Beyle), *Mémoires d'un touriste III, Voyage dans le Midi*, Maspero, 1981.

Tamisier, Christian, 'La forêt en Provence: où sommes-nous et de quoi parle-t-on?', in *Contribution à une réflexion sur le rôle et les usages des bois et collines en basse Provence*, photocopy document (CERFISE, April 1979).

Tiberghien, Gilles A., *Nature, Art, Paysage*, Actes Sud, 2001.

——, *La Nature dans l'Art*, Collection Photo Poche, Actes Sud, 2005.

Tonini, Ida, 'L'Amastuola: Agricultural Landscape Design on a Grand Scale in Puglia', in *The Mediterranean Garden*, No. 65, July 2011, pp. 14–18.

——, 'Giardini di Venezia', in *Rosanova: rivista di arte e storia del giardino*, No. 22, October 2010, pp. 35–57.

——, 'The Jekyll Sisters and the Eden Garden', in *The Mediterranean Garden*, No. 60, April 2010, pp. 14–19.

Tyrwhitt, Mary Jaqueline, *Making a Garden on a Greek Hillside*, Denise Harvey, Greece, 1998.

Verteuil, Anne de, 'Fernando Caruncho', in *Garden Design Journal*, July 2010, Issue 96, pp. 15–18.

Virgil, *Georgics*, Book 1, trans. H. R. Fairclough: see www.theoi.com/Text/VirgilGeorgics1.html#1.

vries, hermann de [sic], *ReConnaître: les choses mêmes, herman de vries, extrait du journal de Digne*, Réserve géologique de Haute-Provence and the Gassendi Museum of Digne, 2001.

Weilacher, Udo, *Between Landscape Architecture and Land Art*, Birkhäuser, 1996; preface by John Dixon Hunt.

Wharton, Edith, *Italian Villas and their Gardens*, Da Capo reprint 1976.

Wilford, John Noble, 'In Syria, a Prologue for Cities', in *The New York Times*, 5 April 2010.

LIST OF ADDRESSES

INTRODUCTION

pp. 7 and 12 Landscape design: Alithea Johns
and Marcus Warren, Skopos Design, Kassiopi,
Corfu 49081, Greece
Tel (+30) 266 308 1996
Email info@skoposdesign.com
Web www.skoposdesign.com

p. 14 Ceràmiques de Santanyí, Calle de la Guàrdia
Civil 22, 07650 Santanyí, Mallorca, Spain
Tel (+34) 971 163 128
Impruneta factory at Impruneta, Tuscany, Italy
Web www.terracottaimpruneta.com

p. 15 Son Bernadinet Hotel, near Campos,
Mallorca
Tel (+34) 971 650 694
Email info@sonbernadinet.com
Web www.son-bernadinet.com

CHAPTER 1 **MOUNTAINS**

Musée Gassendi & Le Cairn Centre d'Art,
04000 Digne-les-Bains, France
Tel (+33) 04 92 31 45 29
Web www.musee-gassendi.org
See also artist herman de vries
Web www.hermandevries.org
See also guide Jean-Pierre Brovelli
Tel (+33) 04 92 35 37 38
Email contact@etoile-rando.com
Web www.etoile-rando.com

Association Sur le Sentier des Lauzes,
Le Villard, 07260 Saint Mélany, France
Tel (+33) 04 75 35 53 92
Email bonjourleslauzes@gmail.com
Web www.surlesentierdeslauzes.fr
See also artist Domingo Cisneros
Web www.territoire.org
See also artist Gilles Clément
Web www.gillesclement.com

CHAPTER 2 **STONEWORKS**

Rou Estate, 49081 Corfu, Greece: owners
Dominic and Claire Skinner
Tel (+30) 697 708 4501
Email info@rouestate.co.uk
Web www.rouestate.co.uk
Landscape design: by the owners and Jennifer
Gay and Piers Goldson
Email jennigay@otenet.gr; piersgoldson@
hotmail.com

Mary Keen and Pip Morrison Designed Landscapes,
The Old Rectory, Duntisbourne Rouse, Glos
GL7 7AP, UK
Tel (+44) 01285 653569 / 07904 388076
Email mary@keengardener.com

Pia Simig, former associate and executor of
the estate of Ian Hamilton Finlay,
Wild Hawthorn Press, The Archive of Ian
Hamilton Finlay, Stonypath, Little Sparta,
Dunsyre, Lanarkshire ML11 8NG, Scotland
Tel (+44) 01899 810252
Email wildhawthornpress@btconnect.co.uk
Web www.ianhamiltonfinlay.com; see also
www.littlesparta.co.uk
The gardens of Fleur de l'Air are not open
to the public.

La Louve, Chemin Saint Gervais, 84480 Bonnieux,
France: owner Judith Pillsbury
Email jinfrance@aol.com
See also www.parcsetjardins.fr
Pool design: Garrett Finney, Farostudio, 3110
Houston Avenue, Houston, Texas 77009, USA
Tel (+1) 713 861 2540
Email info@farostudio.net
Web www.farostudio.net

CHAPTER 3 **EARTHWORKS**

Bibémus Quarry, Route de Vauvenargues,
Aix-en-Provence, France
Web www.aixenprovencetourism.com
Landscape design: Philippe Deliau and Hélène
Bensoam, Atelier Lieux Et Paysages (ALEP),
'La Glaneuse', Avenue Philippe de Girard,
84160 Cadenet, France
Tel (+33) 04 90 68 88 84
Email contact@alep-paysage.com
Web www.alep-paysage.com

Dar Al Hossoun, Sidi Mbarek, Taroudant,
Morocco
Tel (+212) 0528 853 476
Email contact@alhossoun.com
Web www.alhossoun.com
Landscape design: Eric Ossart and Arnaud
Maurières
Web www.maurieres-ossart.com

CHAPTER 4 **WOODWORKS**

For Ian Hamilton Finlay, see Chapter 2

Sheppard Craige, Il Bosco della Ragnaia, Strada
Provinciale 60, San Giovanni d'Asso, Siena, Italy
Email info@laragnaia.com
Web www.laragnaia.com

Jacqueline Morabito, 42/65 rue Yves Klein,
06480 La Colle sur Loup, France
Tel (+33) 04 93 32 64 92
Email jm@jacquelinemorabito.com
Web www.jacquelinemorabito.com

Marc Nucera, BP 16 13550 Noves, France
Tel (+33) 04 90 92 99 21

Domaine de la Verrière, Chemin de la Verrière,
84110 Le Crestet, France
Tel (+33) 06 22 03 31 15
Email info@laverriere.com
Web www.laverriere.com
See also http://chenebleu.wordpress.com

CHAPTER 5 **CLIPPED GREENERY**

For Marc Nucera and Jacqueline Morabito,
see Chapter 4

For La Louve, see Chapter 2

Michel Semini, 2 rue Frusquin, 84220 Goult,
France
Tel (+33) 06 09 52 49 02

Le Jardin des Biehn Maison d'hôtes, 13,
Akbat Sbaa, Douh, 30200 Fes Medina,
Morocco
Tel (+212) 0664 647 679
Email contact@jardindesbiehn.com
Web www.jardindesbiehn.com

Dominique Lafourcade, 10 boulevard Victor Hugo,
13210 Saint Rémy de Provence, France
Tel (+33) 04 90 92 10 14
Email b.lafourcade@wanadoo.fr
Web www.dominique-lafourcade.com

John Rocha, Three Moon Design, Dublin 2,
Ireland
Web www.johnrocha.ie
Landscape design: Benoît Bourdeau,
06500 Menton, France
Tel (+33) 06 79 20 24 75
Web www.benoitbourdeau.com

CHAPTER 6 **MATORRAL, MAQUIS AND MEADOW**

Thomas Doxiadis and Terpsi Kremali,
doxiadis+, 8 Angelou Vlahou St, 10556 Plaka,
Athens, Greece
Tel (+30) 210 677 0662
Email mail@doxiadisplus.com
Web www.doxiadisplus.com

Antiparos Design Properties OLIAROS:
    Iasson Tsakonas, 22 Myllerou St, 104-36 Athens,
    Greece
Tel (+30) 210 523 0417
Email info@oliaros.com
Web www.antiparosdesignproperties.com;
    see also www.oliarosblog.com

deca ARCHITECTURE, 20 Fokylidou,
    106-73 Athens, Greece
Tel (+30) 210 360 3818
Email mailbox@deca.gr
Web www.deca.gr

tala mikdashi
Tel (+44) 020 7373 2875 (London office)
Email tmikdashi@yahoo.com
Web http://talamikdashi.com

Maria Doxa, 1 P. Tsaldari and Tatoiou St, Kifissia,
    145-61 Athens, Greece
Tel (+30) 210 625 3224
Email mail@mariadoxa.gr
Web www.mariadoxa.gr

Paolo Pejrone, Bramafam, 12036 Revello CN, Italy
Tel (+39) 0175 257958
Email arch.pejrone@tiscalinet.it

For the Rou Estate, see Chapter 2

Olivier and Clara Filippi: Pépinière Filippi nursery,
    Plantes pour jardin sec, 34140 Mèze, France
Tel (+33) 04 67 43 88 69
Web www.jardin-sec.com

CHAPTER 7 **FIELD GEOMETRIES**

For Dominique Lafourcade, see Chapter 5

Fernando Caruncho & Asociados, S.L.,
    28707 Madrid, Spain
Tel (+34) 91 657 00 51
Web www.fernandocaruncho.com

CHAPTER 8 **GARDEN**

Mireille Ferrari, Château Malherbe,
    1 route du Bout du Monde,
    83230 Bormes-les-Mimosas, France
Tel (+33) 04 94 64 80 11
Email chateau-malherbe@wanadoo.fr
Web www.chateau-malherbe.com

Giardini Botanici Hanbury (Hanbury
    Botanical Gardens), Corso Montecarlo 43,
    18039 La Mortola Inferiore, Ventimiglia,
    Italy
Tel (+39) 0184 229507
Web www.amicihanbury.com

Giardino di Ninfa, 04013 Cisterna di Latina
    (LT), Italy
Web www.fondazionecaetani.org

For Paolo Pejrone, see Chapter 6

CHAPTER 9 **SEASCAPES**

For the Rou Estate, see Chapter 2

Domaine du Rayol: Le Jardin des Méditerranées,
    Avenue des Belges, 83820 Rayol-Canadel-sur-Mer,
    France
Tel (+33) 04 98 04 44 00
Web www.domainedurayol.org

For Gilles Clément, see Chapter 1

Erik Borja, Domaine des Clairmonts, 26600
    Beaumont-Monteux, France
Tel (+33) 04 75 07 32 27
Email contact@erikborja.fr
Web www.erikborja.fr

CHAPTER 10
EMPORIUM: THE GARDENS OF VENICE

Bauer Palladio, Giudecca 33, 30133 Venice, Italy
Tel (+39) 041 270 3809
Web www.bauerhotels.com

Giuseppe Rallo
Email rallogi@libero.it

Palazzo Soranzo Cappello, Santa Croce 770,
    30100 Venice, Italy
Landscape design: Giuseppe Rallo (see above)
See also www.giardini-venezia.it

CHAPTER 11 **MESURA**
For Ninfa, see Chapter 8

Heidi Gildemeister, E-07460 Pollensa-Mallorca, Spain
Email gilmedit@gmail.com

ACKNOWLEDGMENTS

PICTURE CREDITS

All photographs are by Clive Nichols (www. clivenichols.com) unless otherwise credited. p. 11 Monique Mailloux (www.yriaparos.com); pp. 46, 47, 76 Sam Rebben; pp. 94, 95, 102, 122, 134 (above), 137, 166, 167 (below), 185 (below), 189, 194, 207 Louisa Jones (www.louisajones.fr); p. 123 Olivier Filippi; p. 124 Dario Miale.

AUTHOR'S ACKNOWLEDGMENTS

This book has been in the making for over thirty-five years. I first owe thanks to my husband Bernard Dupont, who has been practising Mediterranean landscape art at home all this time. More recently thanks to my colleague, the photographer Clive Nichols, for his talent, professionalism, rare mix of imagination and practicality, and constant good humour. Many people's reflections, correspondence and conversation have fed my thinking on this subject throughout these years, and many of the same have warmly received me, well beyond the call of duty. I must cite (in alphabetical order): James Aronson, Agnès Brückin, Fernando Caruncho, François Chaslin, Jacques Chibois, Gilles Clément, Yves Delange, Cali Doxiadis and her extended family, Carme Farré, Jean-Laurent Felizia, Olivier Filippi, Garrett Finney, Heidi Gildemeister, Andy Goldsworthy, Nadine Gomez, Kathryn Gustafson, Caroline Harbouri, Alain David Idoux, Merryle Johnson, Mary Keen, Martha Kingsbury, Lucien Kroll, Tania Murray Li, Pierre Lieutaghi, Marguerite Likierman, Nicole Martin Raget, Rick Mather, Arnaud Maurières, Vincent Motte, Jean Mus, Marc Nucera, Eric Ossart, Paolo Pejrone, Pierre Rabhi, Jean-Marie Rey, Pia Simig, Ida Tonini, Nicole de Vésian and William Waterfield. Thanks also to all those journalists and publishers who rarely get named and who work very hard, often in difficult circumstances, to get the very best result possible. Thanks above all to the anonymous Mediterranean gardeners, farmers and craftsmen and women who care about, and care for, the land and keep it fine for future generations.

PHOTOGRAPHER'S ACKNOWLEDGMENTS

I would like to thank my wife and family for putting up with my many trips abroad during the past couple of years, as well as to all the garden owners, designers and artists who feature in this splendid book. Special thanks go to Louisa Jones, not only for her invaluable help with contacts and travel, but also and most importantly for igniting my love affair with Mediterranean gardens and landscapes.

INDEX

Page numbers in *italic* refer to illustrations.

Abbione, Francesco 116
Addison, Joseph 126
Adriatic Sea 164
Aegean region 36, *104*, 164, *108–13*, *167*
Aix-en-Provence, France 58
Al Hossoun, Morocco *54*, *59*, 63, *64–65*, *66*, *67*, *68*, 69
Alaguillaume, Stan 171, *174*
Albania *6*, 39, 40, *165*
ALEP agency 58, 60, 61, *61*
Algiers, Algeria 145
Alpilles, France *82*, 137
Alps *20*, *23*, *27*, 28
Altavès, France *92*
Amastuola, Italy 133
Andalusia, Spain 63, 66, 133
Antiparos *11*, 108–13, *108*, *109*, *110*, *111*, *112*, *112–13*, 115, 180
Ardèche, France *30*, *31*, *32*, *33*
Argentario, Italy 114–19, *114*, *115*, *116*, *117*, *118*, *119*, 180
Ariant, Mallorca *196*, 204–13, *204*, *205*, *206*, *207*, *208*, *209*, *210*, *211*, *212*, *213*
Aristotle 184
Arizona, USA 17
Art Refuges, France 24, 27–28
Asplund, Gunnar 132
Assyria 144
Atlantic Ocean 62, 164
Atlas mountains 62, *62*, 65, 66
Attlee, Helena 149
Auden, W. H. 10, 21, 198
Australia 128
Avlaki Beach, Corfu *167*

Balearic Sea 164
Barba, Javier 42
Barragán, Luis 63, 65
Basra, Iraq 145
Bauer Palladio garden, Italy *187*
Belton, Andy 42
Belton, Karen 42
Belviso, Loïc 177
Bérard, Stéphane 24
Bergé, Pierre 90
Berger, John 128
Bès, River *22*
Bibémus, France 58, *60*, *61*
Biehn, Michel *91*
Blondel, Jacques *6*, *11*, 36, 209
Bonifacio, Corsica 179
Borja, Erik 176–81, *176*, *177*, *178*, *179*, *180*, *181*
Bosc, Hugues 137
Bosco della Ragnaia, Il, Italy 77
Bourdeau, Benoît 102
Bramafam, Italy *122*, 152–55, *153*, *154*, *155*, 158

Braudel, Fernand 10, 22, 63, 145, 183
Brougham, Lord 139
Brovelli, Jean-Pierre 24, 27
Brown, Lancelot 'Capability' 45
Burle Marx, Roberto 63, 115
Burma 68
Byron, Lord 188

Caetani family 146–49, *146*, *147*, *148*, *149*, *150*, *151*, 152, 193, *201*, *202*, *203*: Gelasio Caetani 148, 149; Princess Lelia Caetani 146, 148, 149, 150, 201; Roffredo Caetani 148; *see also* Roffredo Caetani Foundation
Caillois, Roger 139
Cala Rossa, Corsica 176, 180
California, USA 128
Campo, Mallorca *13*, *127*
Canary Islands 39, *171*
Cannes, France 139
Cap Ferrat, France 102
Capri 102, 126
Carmejane, La, France *82*, *84*, *91*, *93*
Caruncho, Fernando *124*, 128, 131–35, *130*, *131*, *132*, *133*, *134*, *135*, *136*, 141, 177
Cavallo, Elio 39
Cazeilles, Adrienne 56
Cézanne, Paul 58, 61
Chénot, Martin 30, 33
Cicero 164
Cisneros, Domingo 30, *30*, *31*
Clément, Gilles 17, 30–33, *32*, *33*, *33*, 168–75, *168*, *169*, *170*, *171*, *172*, *173*, *174*, *175*, 177
Clos Pascal, Le, France *48*, *49*, *89*, *93*
Col de l'Escuichière, France *26*, 27
Columella 71, 80, 122, 144
Confines, Les, France *128*
Conservatoire du Littoral, France 168, 170, 171, 173
Constantinople 194
Corfu *6*, *7*, *12*, *34*, *38*, 39, 45, *75*, 120, 121, *121*, 145, *162*, *164*, *165*, *167*
Corsica *8*, *145*, 164, *166*, 176–81, *177*, *178*, *179*, *180*, *181*
Cotoner family 132
Coxe, Frankie *91*, *93*
Craige, Sheppard 77
Cyclades 108, 111
Cyprus 19

d'Annunzio, Gabriele 185, 192–93
Dante 39, 198
Dar Igdad, Morocco *58*, 69
De Troia, Luca 39
deca ARCHITECTURE *108*, *111*
Delacroix, Eugène 58
Deliau, Philippe 58, *60*, *61*, 171
Desplats, Christian 173
Digne-les-Bains, France 22, 23, 24, 27, *27*, *29*, 33
Dion, Mark 24
Domaine de la Malherbe, France *142*, 156–61, *156–57*, *157*, *158*, *159*, *160*, *161*

Domaine de la Verrière, France *82*, *85*
Domaine des Clairmonts, France *176*, *176–77*
Domaine du Rayol, France 30, 168–75, *168*, *169*, *170*, *171*, *172*, *173*, *174*, *175*, 180
Dompnac, France 33
Doxa, Maria *109*, *113*
doxiadis+ agency 17, *104*, *106*, 108, *108*, *109*, *110*, *111*, 112, *112*, *112–13*
Doxiadis, Cali 121
Doxiadis, Thomas 108, 112
Drobie valley, France 30
Durrell, Lawrence 19, 125
Duse, Eleanora 193

Eden, Caroline 191, 193
Eden, Frederick 188, 189, 191, 193, 201
Egypt 44, 144, 163
England 80, 146, 200
Etruria, Italy 39

Ferrari, Mireille *142*, 156–61, *156–57*, *157*, *158*, *159*, *160*, *161*
Filippi, Olivier and Clara 121, *123*
Finlay, Ian Hamilton 45–50, *46*, *47*, 74, *76*, *77*, 79
Finney, Garrett 15, 50, *52–53*
Fleur de l'Air, France 45, 47, *46*, *47*, *76*, 77
Fontcuberta, Joan 24
Fortescue, Lady 120–21
France 14, *16*, 30, 106, 107, 121, 128, 200

Garcin, Emile *92*
Gassendi, Pierre 24
Gay, Jennifer 45
Germany 120
Gette, Paul-Armand 24, 33
Ghika, Barbara 40
Ghika, Nicolas 40
Gibraltar, Straits of 164
Gildemeister, Heidi 204–13, *204*, *205*, *206*, *207*, *208*, *209*, *210*, *211*, *212*, *213*
Gilpin, William 72
Giono, Jean 14, 22, 35, 58, 79, 163
Goldson, Piers 45
Goldsworthy, Andy *20*, 22–25, 27–28, *27*, 30, 33, 42
Gomez, Nadine 23–24, 33
Gordes, France *44*
Gormley, Antony 28, 33
Grasse, France 209
Graves, Robert 44
Graves, William 44
Greece 17, 88, *104*, 106, *106*, 108–13, 115, 116, 164
Grotto Garden, Corfu 42
Grove, The, France *77*, *78*, *79*, 100, 101, *103*

Hamlet, The, France *98*, *99*
Hanbury Botanical Gardens, Italy *144*
Hannibal 22
Harbouri, Caroline 88, 173
Harbouri, Petrie 58

Hesiod 164, 197, 209
Highet, Gilbert 6
Hills, Paul 185, 186, 191
Homer 39, 49, 94, 120, 144
Horden, Peregrine 13, 14, 19, 72, 74, 141, 145, 180, 184, 210
Hortus Unicorni, Italy 39
Hôtel de la Mer, France 168, 171, 175
Howard, Esme 148
Howard, Hubert 148, 150
Hunt, John Dixon 19, 45, 48, 79, 185, 188, 193, 194
Huxley, Aldous 74, 80

Idoux, Alain David 81, 81, 137–41, 136, 138, 139, 140
Ischia, Italy 185
Israel 106
Italy 106, 115, 116, 124, 126, 133, 144, 146–55, 200

James, Henry 186, 191, 192, 194, 200
Japan 176–81
Jekyll, Gertrude 193

Kanonas, Corfu 39–40, 42, 42, 43
Keen, Mary 39–43
Kew, England 42
Kingsbury, Martha 105
Klein, Eric 24
Kremali, Terpsi 108

La Mortola, Italy 144
Lafourcade, Dominique 93, 126, 128, 128
Laguna, Guillaume 138
Languedoc, France 123
Lazio, Italy 146, 147, 148, 149, 150, 151, 201, 202, 203
Le Corbusier (Charles-Édouard Jeanneret) 101
Lebanon 63
Lejeune, Jean-François 102
Lepini hills, Italy 149
Lévi-Strauss, Claude 17
Little Sparta, Scotland 45
Lloyd, Christopher 95
Louve, La, France 15, 50, 50, 51, 52, 52–53, 53, 94–96, 94, 95, 96, 137
Luberon, France 94

Madagascar 68
Mallorca 9, 13, 14, 15, 36, 44, 56, 56–57, 57, 127, 131–33, 130, 131, 132, 132, 133, 134, 135, 145, 204–13, 204, 205, 206, 207, 208, 209, 210, 211, 212, 213
Malta 39
Manrique, César 39
Marchetti, Lauro 101, 146, 148, 152, 157, 160, 201, 203
Marchetti, Stella 160, 203
Marrakech, Morocco 63, 65
Martin, Etienne 24
Martineau, Alice 44
Mas de Benoît, France 136, 137–41, 136, 138, 139, 140, 141

Mas de Michel, France 82, 137
Mas du Baraquet, France 93, 126
Mas Vincent, France 90
Maurières, Arnaud 63–69, 63, 64–65, 66, 67, 68, 69
Menton, France 171
Mesopotamia 44
Mexico 68
Mèze, France 123
Michelet, Jules 46, 50
Midwest, American 120
mikdashi, tala 109, 113
Mont Sainte-Victoire, France 58, 61
Mont Ventoux, France 82
Montaigne, Michel de 136
Morabito, Jacqueline 77–79, 77, 78, 79, 84, 98–103, 98, 99, 100, 103
Morocco 54, 58, 59, 62–69, 145
Mus, Jean 128
Musée Branly gardens, France 30

Napoleon Bonaparte 188, 189
Nash, David 84
Nice, France 102
Ninfa, Italy 101, 146–51, 146, 147, 148, 149, 150, 151, 152, 157–59, 193, 198, 199, 201–3, 201
Nobel, Alfred 171
Nonas, Richard 24, 210
Nucera, Marc 70, 80, 80–85, 80, 81, 82, 83, 84, 85, 86, 198, 97, 97, 137, 137, 138

OLIAROS development 104, 106, 108–13, 108, 109, 110, 111, 112, 112–13
Ossart, Eric 63–69, 63, 64–65, 66, 67, 68, 69

Page, Russell 115, 149, 158, 160
Palazzo Soranzo Cappello, Italy 189, 192–93, 192, 193
Papanek, Victor 13, 49
Parc André Citroën, France 30
Parco di Celle, Italy 77
Paris, France 30, 94, 176
Paros 107, 108
Paulille, France 171
Pearson, Dan 88, 101
Pejrone, Paolo 114–19, 121, 144, 152–55, 153, 154, 155, 160
Peninsula Garden, Corsica 177, 179, 180, 181
Penone, Giuseppe 6, 55, 84
Petit, Caroline 171
Petrarch 198
Picasso, Christine 80
Piedmont, Italy 24, 122, 152–55, 153, 154, 155, 210
Pillsbury, Judy 15
Pistoia, Italy 77
Pitte, Jean-Robert 127
Pliny the Elder 146
Pliny the Younger 126, 128
Po valley 145
Polo, Marco 194
Pontikonisi, Corfu 167

Porto Vecchio, Corsica 166
Provence, France 14, 15, 18, 20, 22, 22, 24, 24, 25, 26, 27, 29, 37, 39, 44, 45, 46, 47, 47, 48, 49, 50, 51, 52–53, 53, 58, 60, 61, 70, 73, 74, 76, 77, 79, 80, 80, 81, 82, 82, 83, 84, 85, 86, 89, 90, 91, 92, 93, 94, 95, 96, 97, 121, 126, 128, 136, 137, 137, 138, 139, 140, 141, 163, 210
Puglia, Italy 124, 133
Purcell, Nicholas 13, 14, 19, 72, 74, 141, 145, 180, 184, 210

Quest-Ritson, Charles 146, 149, 201

Rackham, Oliver 11
Rallo, Giuseppe 187, 189, 192, 192–93
Renaud, David 24
Rey, Jean-Marie 97
Rhône valley 58, 177
Richardson, Tim 126
Riviera 44, 77, 78, 79, 98–103, 98, 99, 100, 102, 103, 121, 139, 142, 156–57, 157, 158, 159, 160, 161, 168, 169, 170, 171, 172, 174, 175, 180
Rocha, John 102, 102–03
Roche-Rousse, La, France 28
Roffredo Caetani Foundation 146, 150
Rome, Italy 74, 115, 129, 144, 145, 146
Romilly, Jacqueline de 58
Rothschild family 39–40, 40, 41, 42, 43: Beth Rothschild 40, 41, 42; Emmy Rothschild 42
Rou Estate, Corfu 34, 38, 45, 120, 121, 162, 164
Rousseau, Jean-Jacques 131
Roussillon, France 166, 171

Sa Vina Vella, Mallorca 130, 131–35, 131, 132, 133, 134, 135
Sabatino, Michelangelo 102
Sahara desert 62, 68, 69
Saint-Régis, chapel of, France 33
Saint-Symphorien, Prieuré, France 39, 73
Saint-Tropez, France 94, 156, 168
Scarpa, Carlo 198
Scotland 45, 47, 50
Scott, Geoffrey 150
Semini, Michel 90, 128
Sentier des Lauzes, France 16, 30–33, 31, 32, 33
Serre de la Madone, France 171
Serres, Olivier de 143
Sicily 63
Simig, Pia 45
Skinner, Dom 34
Skopos agency 12
Smithson, Robert 16, 47
Smollett, Tobias 209
Spain 101, 106, 144
Stendhal (Marie-Henri Beyle) 74
Strabo 184
Strongilo, Corfu 39–42
Studio Lazzarini Pickering 115
Syria 63

Tamisier, Christian 72
Taroudant, Morocco 62, *62*, 63, 65
Terrain, Le, France *83, 85*
Tiberghien, Gilles 16, 18
Timothy Hatton Associates 40
Tonini, Ida 185, 186, 193, 194
Toulon, France 80, 168
Trabari, France *37, 74, 97*
Tsakonas, Iasson 108
Tunisia 68
Turrell, James 17
Tuscany, Italy *14*, 77, 114–19, *114, 115, 116, 117, 118, 119*

Urquijo, Pablo Carvajal 132

Van Gogh, Vincent 58
Vaucluse, France 39
Venice, Italy 19, 39, 182–95, *182, 183, 184, 185, 186, 187, 188, 189, 190, 191, 192, 193, 194, 195*, 201
Vésian, Nicole de 15, 36, 48–51, *48, 49, 50, 51, 52–53, 53, 73, 74*, 77, 81, 82, *88, 89, 93*, 94–97, *94, 95*, 98, 101, 137, *137*, 138
Vieil Esclangon, France *20, 24, 25*, 27, 28
Vière, France 24, 210
Villa Savoie, France 101

Vilmouth, Jean-Luc 24
Virgil 49, 107, 148
Vlacherna, Greece *167*
vries, herman de 24, 28, *29*

Weilacher, Udo 17
Wharton, Edith 87, 91, 139
Wisley, England 149
Woodland Chapel, Sweden 132